WALK
AWAY
WEALTHY

THE ENTREPRENEUR'S
EXIT-PLANNING PLAYBOOK

MARK M. TEPPER, CFP®

GREENLEAF
BOOK GROUP PRESS

Published by Greenleaf Book Group Press
Austin, Texas
www.gbgpress.com

Distributed by Greenleaf Book Group LLC

For ordering information or special discounts for bulk purchases, please contact Greenleaf Book Group LLC at PO Box 91869, Austin, TX 78709, 512.891.6100.

Design and composition by Greenleaf Book Group LLC
Cover design by Greenleaf Book Group LLC

Publisher's Cataloging-In-Publication Data

Tepper, Mark M., 1980- , author.
  Walk away wealthy : the entrepreneur's exit-planning playbook / Mark M. Tepper, CFP.—First edition.
    pages ; cm
  Issued also as an ebook.
  ISBN: 978-1-62634-084-8
  1. Sale of business enterprises. 2. Businesspeople—Finance, Personal. I. Title.
HD1393.25 .T466 2014
658.1/64   2014931799

Part of the Tree Neutral® program, which offsets the number of trees consumed in the production and printing of this book by taking proactive steps, such as planting trees in direct proportion to the number of trees used: www.treeneutral.com

TreeNeutral

Printed in the United States of America on acid-free paper

14 15 16 17 18 19   10 9 8 7 6 5 4 3 2 1

First Edition

To my EO Forum mates, my clients, the Strategic Wealth Partners team, and most of all my family—my heartfelt thanks.

CONTENTS

PART III: *Preserving Value*

FOREWORD

Grab a copy of the Forbes 400, the magazine's list of the richest people in America, and you'll see the following surnames at the top: Gates, Buffett, Ellison, Koch, Walton, and Bloomberg.

There isn't a single movie star in the top ten. Nor is there even one professional athlete, rock star, lottery winner, or TV personality. In fact, the Forbes 400 list is made up almost entirely of entrepreneurs and their heirs.

There is simply no better way to become wealthy in America than starting and successfully exiting a business. Merrill Lynch estimates that 80 percent of the high-net-worth (HNW) people they target—those investors with at least $5 million of investable assets—are former business owners who have enjoyed a "liquidity event."

So it is correct to say that the vast majority of HNW investors are entrepreneurs, but that is not the same thing as saying that all entrepreneurs are wealthy. In fact, most owners are "business rich" and relatively cash poor. They have the majority of their wealth tied up in an illiquid asset that may or may not be worth something one day in the future. According to our research over at The Sellability Score, seven in ten business owners say they want to exit in the next ten years, yet only one in ten have an exit plan written down.

So if you're an entrepreneur and your goal is to become wealthy, you're riding the right horse. But whether that horse wins the Kentucky Derby or comes up lame has everything to do with your exit plan.

The trick to a successful exit is to understand what makes your business valuable to an investor. In *Walk Away Wealthy,* Mark Tepper does a great job of outlining what entrepreneurs need to think about when planning for the day they hit the eject button.

As Mark points out, planning an exit requires that you look at your business through a new lens. Most owners think about how to grow their revenue and profits, but preparing a business to sell also demands that you look at your business through the eyes of an acquirer and think about what drives value for them.

In fact, what makes your business profitable from one year to the next may be at odds with what makes it valuable. Purchasing new customer relationship management software will cut into this year's profits, but it will make for a more valuable company down the road. Likewise, hiring a salesperson to replace yourself as a rainmaker will make your business less profitable in the short term but much more valuable in the long run.

Read on and you'll get a treasure trove of wisdom from an entrepreneur and financial advisor who knows what it takes to create a business that is "built to sell."

And it will take you closer to whatever list you might be striving for!

John Warrillow
Founder of The Sellability Score and author of *Built to Sell: Creating a Business That Can Thrive Without You*

INTRODUCTION

Those who are unwilling to invest in the future haven't earned one.
—H. W. LEWIS, TECHNOLOGICAL RISK

When you launched your business, whether it was two years ago or twenty-five years ago, you probably planned on selling it sometime in the future—preferably for a load of money. Millions of business owners around the United States share the same goal: cash out and use the proceeds of the sale to fund the hobbies, travel, and family time they had to put on hold in order to focus on running their company. That may be your dream as well.

Dreams are terrific, but selling a business isn't easy. Even if you can do it, you won't necessarily gain lifelong financial freedom. So while an entrepreneur about to launch his company might give himself a pep talk about selling in twenty years for

$10 million and retiring to a beach house on Maui, the reality is sobering. For example:

» Based on my experience, only 20 percent of businesses for sale will successfully transfer to another owner. The other 80 percent will transfer to family members, be taken over by employees, or cease to exist, usually because the owner doesn't have any other options. While some might consider transferring their business to the next generation a successful outcome, it rarely produces a payout comparable to what may be realized by selling to a third party. If your business does more than $2 million in annual revenues, your odds improve to about 30 percent, but that's still nothing to write home about.

» According to the 2013 Q3 BizBuySell Insight Report, the average sale price for a small business was $180,000 with a multiple of 0.6.[1] That means the average small business sold for only 60 percent of the value of EBITDA (earnings before interest, taxes, depreciation, and amortization, the standard measure of a company's cash flow). That's a rude wake-up call for an owner who assumes that selling for four or five times EBITDA is inevitable.

» According to the 2010–2011 PriceWaterhouseCoopers Family Business Survey, 55 percent of family business owners expect to sell their businesses to another company, a private equity firm or a management team within the next five years. However, only half of those owners have a succession plan.[2]

Despite these alarming facts, many owners stubbornly cling to fantasies about selling their businesses easily and for big money. They're certain that they will (a) find multiple high-quality suitors for their company as soon as they put it on the market; (b) get several quick offers worth many times their company's EBITDA; and (c) walk away rich and happy without having done any serious exit planning in advance.

Maybe it's a fascination with Wall Street stock offerings or an emotional attachment to the thing they've built that makes millions of entrepreneurs behave so irrationally. But the reason doesn't matter. If you want to achieve your goal of successfully selling your company on *your* terms, for *your* price, according to *your* timetable, you can't think like they do. If you want to defy the odds, there's an essential strategy you must follow that will dramatically improve your chances of a successful sale:

Put a strong exit plan in place.

Exit planning should be an integral part of your business plan. In fact, if possible, it should be part of your startup plan. Building with your eventual exit in mind will lead you to make decisions that increase the long-term value of your company: hiring and training top-flight managers, streamlining systems and processes, broadening your client base, protecting your intellectual property, and putting together a team of experienced financial professionals.

By keeping your exit in your sights, you'll be encouraged to make your company more efficient, better able to run without your hands-on involvement, and more profitable. That's what buyers are looking for. Buyers of small businesses (broadly defined here as companies with $5 million or less in gross annual revenues) and midmarket companies ($5 million–plus in gross annual revenues) are hunting for well-run, sustainable businesses that either fill a niche in their portfolios or can be grown and sold at a profit. If your company doesn't fit that description, they'll buy somebody else's.

So, would you rather be one of the 80 percent who don't succeed in selling their business—or the 20 percent who do?

MY EXPERTISE

In *Walk Away Wealthy*, I'm going to give you a crash course in exit planning and financial planning that's specific to entrepreneurs—one that you can finish in the time it takes to fly nonstop from Los Angeles to New York. I'm going to share the secrets I've discovered after spending years helping the owners of closely held businesses set up first-rate exit plans and execute successful sales, employee buyouts, and family transfers.

For the last several years, I've been a member of Entrepreneurs' Organization (EO) and enjoyed the opportunity to serve on the board of my local chapter. EO is a network of more than eight thousand business owners worldwide that enables and inspires entrepreneurs to learn from one another, leading to greater success in business and in personal life. In my discussions with my fellow entrepreneurs within EO, I have found the topic of exit planning to be of the utmost importance. Based on my observations, however, many entrepreneurs are neglecting their own exit planning, in part because there appears to be a dearth of quality information on the subject.

That is what inspired me to put together *Walk Away Wealthy*. The intention of this book is to provide you with enough information on exit planning that you can take the right steps with the right people on your team, ensuring that you make the most of what will be the most significant financial event of your lifetime—your exit from your business.

As a CERTIFIED FINANCIAL PLANNER™ professional (also known as a *CFP® professional*), I specialize in creating personal financial strategies for entrepreneurs—strategies that center on the successful transfer of their most valuable asset. I work closely with the other key exit-planning professionals—certified public accountants, investment bankers, and mergers and acquisitions (M&A) attorneys—to develop strategies that maximize both a company's sellability and its owner's potential financial reward, including tax planning, estate planning, and a plan for establishing a steady, growing cash flow.

The most successful exits require proactive, advance planning. A well-constructed exit plan addresses the following areas:

1. *Determining exit objectives.* What constitutes, in your mind, a successful exit? When do you want to walk away from the business? What kind of annual income do you need in your post-work life to enjoy the lifestyle you want? Who is your choice to run the business after you're gone? Do you have secondary objectives, such as taking care of valuable employees?

2. *Assessing your current financial condition.* How much is your business worth? What kind of income can you expect from sources unrelated to the sale of your business, such as funds in retirement accounts? Will your combined sources of income be enough to sustain the lifestyle you want?

3. *Determining the best ways to increase the sellable value of your business.* Once you know the market value of your business, what are the best ways to increase the value of your equity? How can you mitigate risks and make your company more attractive to a prospective buyer? What can you do to ensure that your business does not lose value between now and your exit?

4. *Implementing tax minimization strategies.* Taxes can dramatically impact the size of your "liquidity event" (as the pros call it) and even leave you with insufficient income to fund your retirement. Is your company incorporated in a way that

allows for optimal tax reduction? What kind of deal should you be looking for to reduce your tax burden?

5. *Considering options for transferring your business.* Are you considering transferring your business to family members, co-owners, or employees? Do you know how to do it without losing control of the business until you have all of your cash and while paying the least possible taxes?

6. *Considering options for selling.* Do you know how to sell your business to a third party? How will you find your buyer? What represents a good deal? Who should handle due diligence and negotiations? How can you maximize your cash while reducing your tax liability?

7. *Preparing for the unexpected.* Do you have a business continuity plan? What have you done to ensure that the business continues if you die, become disabled, or simply decide to walk away? Have you provided for your family's financial well-being should you die or become incapacitated before *or* after your exit?

Doing all this takes time, which is another reason that I counsel my clients to begin exit planning as early as they can. Implementing the many changes that make a company worth more money to a prospective buyer takes years; you can't wake up one morning, slap your hand to your forehead, and cry, "Good grief, I need to sell my company in six months!" and expect to get good results. Hiring the best people and putting in place sustainable, profit-generating processes are often a matter of trial and error, and you can't do them overnight.

Walk Away Wealthy is intended for privately held small business and midmarket company owners who

» are considering an exit from their companies within the next five years, whether that means selling to an outside buyer or pursuing such options as transferring the company to their family members or selling it to employees;

» know they should be doing some exit planning but haven't done much to prepare for their liquidity event; and

» realize that it's time to stop procrastinating and start putting people and systems in place to ensure a smooth, profitable exit.

Don't be embarrassed if you haven't done any real exit planning up to now; you're not alone. From this point on, however, your mission is to make your eventual exit your most important business objective. Selling your business will more than likely be the most significant financial event of your lifetime. It only happens once, and if you screw it up, you don't get a do-over. Properly planning for this event will help you hire smarter. It will help you reduce your personal work hours by building a sustainable company that's able to operate independently of you. It will help you be more efficient in your business practices and operations, which will improve profitability. And it will prepare you for when an offer comes out of the blue. Simply put, focusing on your future will also improve your present.

WHAT'S INSIDE

I've broken down exit planning into twelve secrets that most business owners don't know or refuse to believe, divided into three areas:

1. *Building value*—Secrets for increasing what your business is worth

2. *Monetizing value*—Secrets that help you find the right buyer and get the best offer

3. *Preserving value*—Secrets that help you keep more of the amount you make in your sale

Each of these three areas is further divided into four distinct secrets that will help you plan your exit from your business so you can walk away wealthy. In each section, I'll debunk some of the common misconceptions about exiting a business, such as the *I don't need experts—I can sell my company myself* myth. (Note: Trying to sell your company on your own is generally a terrible idea.) Next, I'll bring you up to speed on sound exit planning, by sharing the secret strategies that smart entrepreneurs (and their advisory teams) use to sell their companies for more money and walk away satisfied with the transaction. Finally, I'll tell you exactly what to do next, step by step, to move forward with your own exit strategy.

But suppose you *did* wake up this morning, slap your hand to your forehead, and cry, "Good grief, I need to sell my company in six months!" Not to worry. You can't make up for the lost years during which you could have been developing your exit plan, but you can take steps to capitalize on your opportunities and get the best financial return possible. Each of the twelve secrets includes a sidebar called "Exit 911" featuring a critical, do-or-die tip for the owner who hopes to exit his or her business in twelve months or less. If you follow my Exit 911 tips and do nothing else, you'll still increase your chances of selling successfully and walking away wealthier.

YOUR SELLABILITY SCORE

Finally, before we dig into the secrets of a successful exit, I want to invite you to visit www.swpconnect.com (the website of my company, Strategic Wealth Partners) and get your Sellability Score. If you're wondering how viable your business could be in the mergers and acquisitions market *right now*, the Sellability Score is a great tool to help you find out.

Start by completing a free online questionnaire that weighs dozens of variables to gauge your business's value on the open market using a score between 1 and 100. Answering the questions takes only fifteen to twenty minutes. The report I'll send to your email inbox will tell you how sellable your company is today, based on eight key areas that determine value. Not to mention that the report is like an MBA course in selling a business! For instance, did you know that when buyers value your business, many will "discount" your projected future profits by their desired rate of return—say, 15 percent? The higher that rate, the riskier your business . . . and the lower the purchase price. That's insider information most entrepreneurs don't have a clue about. It comes with your Sellability Score.

Okay, enough preamble. You have a business to run, and I have secrets to share. I'll leave you with this thought: No matter how little attention you've paid to exit planning up to this point, it's never too late to take positive, meaningful steps. Doing so will only improve your business—and your future. Best of luck!

PART I

BUILDING VALUE

CREATE YOUR EXIT PLAN BEFORE YOU NEED IT

Investing should be more like watching paint dry or watching grass grow. If you want excitement, take $800 and go to Las Vegas.
—PAUL SAMUELSON, ECONOMIST

THE FACTS

Peter Alternative is an investment banker with Mirus Capital Advisors in Burlington, Massachusetts. One day, he polled a group of entrepreneurs working with the Massachusetts Institute of Technology Enterprise Forum and found that for every twenty entrepreneurs he surveyed, fifteen had received unsolicited offers for their businesses.

That's not surprising. In my experience, if you're running a successful business, you are very likely to receive an unsolicited offer at some point. What I do find surprising about Peter's account, however, is the fact that not a single one of the entrepreneurs he surveyed had a cohesive plan in place for responding appropriately to the offers they received.

You can chalk that up to a lack of exit planning, something that is a huge problem for most business owners. If you get an unsolicited offer for your company next Thursday and you don't have a comprehensive exit plan, what will you do? Will you know if the offer reflects an accurate open market value of your company? If you accept, will you soon find yourself improvising your legal strategy and tax planning? That's a recipe for financial disaster.

Unfortunately, not all entrepreneurs see the value in early exit planning. In fact, when it comes to exit planning, I've found that entrepreneurs fall into two basic camps:

1. Those who treat their businesses as investments and make decisions that build sustainable long-term value, including putting a solid exit plan in place

2. Those who operate their businesses as cash-generating engines to fund their lifestyles, with little or no thought or planning beyond the next quarter

If you are part of the first group, you're already doing many of the things that will increase your company's long-term value. If you got an offer from a prospective buyer tomorrow, you'd be much better prepared to negotiate an attractive deal. If you're in the second group (which is much larger), then it's unlikely that you have even given more than a passing thought to your exit strategy. You're not thinking for the long term, so you haven't designed your company to grow sustainably over the years. You could be squandering millions of dollars in potential company value.

Sound exit planning will increase the value of your business in a buyer's eyes. Despite this, many entrepreneurs believe the myth that they can put off exit planning until they are "ready to sell," whenever that is. *Big mistake.* Procrastinating leaves them unprepared not just for an out-of-the-blue offer but for an orderly exit on their preferred terms. These entrepreneurs are not in a position to understand how an offer impacts their sale price, tax burden, or future wealth. And they lack the knowledge to negotiate effectively with a potential buyer. More than a few owners have been forced to turn away an offer because they didn't have their ducks in a row, only to find out the hard way that it was the *only* offer they would ever receive.

It's not difficult to understand why many entrepreneurs are reluctant to think about exit planning at the beginning of the business life cycle. When you launch your company, you spend most of your time in survival mode, doing whatever you can to generate income and keep the lights on. Planning for your exit seems like a frivolous waste of time. Entrepreneurs also ignore exit planning because of other misconceptions:

» They assume that when they are ready to sell, a buyer will appear.

» They don't understand the complexity of selling a business.

» They don't like thinking about retirement or mortality.

» They assume they will just pass the company on to their kids or sell to a group of employees.

But the most common problem may be that entrepreneurs think about their exit as an isolated event—they accept an offer, get a check, and book their flight to Bermuda. But an exit is not an event; it's a process that can take at least two to three years—a process that should continually be subjected to revision and updating. Creating your exit plan should be a time-intensive process; this is a dynamic situation, not a static plan. You don't have to create the plan again and again into perpetuity, but it will need to be recalibrated and fine-tuned as the facts change. The most successful businesses are those whose owners view them as an investment—and thus begin the exit-planning process as soon as possible.

If you view your eventual exit not as an ongoing invest-ment but as a disconnected moment in time, you won't take the long view of your company's development. You're more likely to neglect the strategies that build long-term value—and value is what brings the life-changing payout, the pot of gold at the end of the rainbow.

Like it or not, exiting your business is inevitable. You'd better plan for it, because ignoring it will cost you. As a fictional example, let's say that in 2012, Jim Smith told his financial advisor he wanted to leave his company in five years by selling it for enough cash to live comfortably post-exit. The advisor saw that yearly cash flow was around $1.5 million, while the company's value was estimated to be around $6 million. Jim's salary—of $600,000—came out of annual cash flow.

Jim and his advisor set about increasing the company's value, decreasing taxes, and maintaining the existing value, but they never got down to creating an actual exit strategy.

After five years, Jim's company had only changed for the worse. A recession had impeded cash flow, and Jim was getting discouraged about the prospect of selling. He hadn't done anything to improve cash flow through the difficult period, nor had he documented and updated his business systems. His leadership team hadn't been restructured, and this under-motivated group had little chance of keeping the company running after Jim was gone. It looked like Jim was looking at another five years.

That's why it's so critical to begin the planning process as early as possible in the life cycle of your business. When you wait until there's an offer on the table, there's no way to put that time back on the clock.

THE SECRET

If you want to sell your business for the highest possible value, begin looking at your business as an investment in your ideal future—not as a job that you've created for yourself—and start developing your exit strategy as soon as possible. If you can, start today. It's never too late to put a smart exit plan in place, provided that you begin planning *now*.

No buyer wants to purchase a job. Buyers want an investment that will increase in value while providing predictable, growing cash flow over the long term. Designing your business to do both makes it more likely that a buyer will see it as a valuable, sustainable source of profits that is worth paying a substantial amount to acquire.

Adopting this investment-based view will change the way you see your company. It will enable you to develop your business model in such a way that you can weave value-creating strategies into the business organically. These big-picture strategies become just a normal part of how you run things.

Here are some important steps you can take in planning for your exit:

> » *Find the heart of your exit team.* You'll need a certified public accountant (CPA) and a CFP® professional who have managed multiple successful owner exits. (I'll explain later

why a CFP® professional is likely your best choice.) Selling a business is extremely complex and will impact your tax burden and wealth for the rest of your life. While you may never have sold a business before, an experienced CPA or CFP® professional will have presided over numerous sales and transfers. With these advisors on your team—people who will become as familiar with your business as you are—you'll be better equipped to set sound goals, enact systems that will increase the company's value, and make business decisions based on facts, not emotions.

You may already have relationships with a CPA and a financial advisor. But if they don't have experience selling businesses, consider replacing them now with experienced people. You'll avoid having to replace them later in the process.

» *Develop an operational model that keeps the company running smoothly with minimal daily involvement from you.* Some entrepreneurs fail to find buyers because they spend years working *in* their businesses while not working *on* them. They're neck-deep in every department and every transaction; nothing moves without their say-so. While this can be satisfying for the ego, it's poison for the bank account. From the outset, a smart owner puts in place people, technology, and processes that encourage the business to grow even when he or she is not part of everyday operations. This makes the business more attractive to buyers who aren't interested in buying *you* along with your company.

» *Balance today's need for comfort with tomorrow's demand for value.* Some businesses wind up becoming little more than an ATM designed to generate cash flow to fund their owner's lifestyle. Revenues go to cover payments for luxury cars, country club membership fees, family vacations, and the like. There's nothing wrong with any of those things; if you're going to work an entrepreneur's long hours, you deserve some R & R. But some decisions that increase cash flow in the present—such as taking on lucrative but resource-draining clients, giving away patents and trademarks, or going for cheap benefits packages that cripple your ability to attract the best people—can conflict with your real goal: building sellable value in the long term.

» *Develop your personal exit plan, and build your company to serve that plan.* Do you know your "number"—the amount of money you'll need to fund your dream retirement? If you want to pass your company to your heirs, how will you ensure that they are ready to run it? What will you do with all that time you currently put into your business? Transferring your company brings up questions about investing, taxation, lifestyle, family, and even your life's purpose. Knowing your goals and asking critical questions early on allows you to develop a business model that serves your financial, family, and personal goals.

HOW YOU'LL BENEFIT

There's no benefit to be had by delaying the exit-planning process until you are "ready," whereas there is nothing but benefit to be gained by starting now. By following a business model designed to grow sustainable value over a ten- or twenty-year time frame, you'll build a stronger, more profitable, more valuable company that demands less of your time today.

A perfect example of this is the company built by Tim Nguyen. Tim is a thirty-two-year-old wunderkind who founded InHouse Solutions, which provides real estate valuation services and software to mortgage lending services around the United States. In ten years, he has built a sixty-five-employee business with about $20 million in annual revenues, but he's designed the company with such efficiency and such an eye toward his eventual exit that he works only about one hour per week.

This arrangement has let Tim do something that would turn most entrepreneurs green with envy: keep his company and enjoy the comfortable lifestyle and charitable work that it funds, without feeling as though he's chained to his office desk. He has planned his exit so well that now he doesn't *need* to exit—he is already realizing personal freedom and financial independence.

"When I started the company, I didn't know anything," Tim says. "Through the process of building it and planning to sell, I realized that I didn't know how to run it. When you don't know what you're doing, you work a lot and you get very tired. You can't wait to get out. Now that I know how to run the company, things are different."

His secret? "Most small businesses grow only to the size of their owners' egos," he says. "You have to let go of your ego. You have to realize that there are people in the world who are smarter than you, work harder than you, and can achieve more than you. My job is to attract the right people, provide the resources they need, remove obstacles, and get out of the way. I don't get involved in strategy anymore."[3]

Tim estimates that by 2025, InHouse Solutions could sell for $500 million. His experience demonstrates a core principle of smart exit planning: The best way to build value in your company is to build something that operates so flawlessly, with so little effort on your part, that you don't want to sell it. Those are the businesses that will command the highest multiple.

Whether or not you see yourself holding on to your business for the next few years, there are plenty of other good reasons to start exit planning today:

» *You'll know your business's sellability.* Wanting to sell your company doesn't mean an investor will be interested in buying it. By planning in advance, you and your team will find out if your business has sellable value. If it doesn't, you can choose to make changes that increase value, or you can leave things as they are and make other plans to fund your retirement. Either way, you're not flying blind.

» *You won't fear the ups and downs of the mergers and acquisitions market.* The M&A market (the market for buying and selling privately held companies) tends to run in three-to-five-year cycles, during which multiples and valuations expand and contract depending on the stage of the cycle. If the time comes to sell and the market is in a trough, you won't get the amount you want. Sometimes, a successful exit isn't about when *you're* ready; it's about when the *market* is ready. When you have an exit plan in place, you can entertain offers when the M&A market is hot and accept a great offer even if it comes a few years early.

» *You'll hold the power when negotiating.* Some entrepreneurs jump at the first unsolicited offer that comes along, even if it's not very good, because they haven't done their homework. They don't know what the business should sell for, but they know they haven't optimized its value. They fear that nobody else will ask them to the prom, so they take the first offer—and wind up getting less than their business is worth. But having a realistic multiple supported by solid data puts you in the driver's seat when an offer comes in. You can either decline a poor offer or negotiate a higher price from a position of strength.

» *You'll have more exit options.* Maybe you don't want to cash out. Maybe your dream is to pass your company on to your children. That's great. But a successful transfer doesn't happen overnight. You need to plan for the tax implications. You need to set up the financing. You need to make sure your heirs possess the interest and skills required to run the company. It takes years to put those pieces in place. Start now.

» *You'll be prepared for the unexpected.* I've talked about positioning your company to its full advantage to get the most from an unsolicited offer. But what if some hardship befalls you? What happens if you are disabled in an accident and can't work? Who has legal authority to manage your company? Who else knows how to keep it running profitably? Your exit blueprint should include a clear succession plan and an organizational strategy that leaves the company able to function smoothly without you.

» *You'll get more money at closing.* I've seen cases where smart, proactive exit planning doubled—yes, *doubled*—the value of a company's liquidity event versus a comparable business that didn't do any planning. When the owner builds with the exit in mind, the company becomes more stable, sustainable, and valuable to quality buyers.

WHAT TO DO

1. Determine what your endgame looks like, whether it's a sale to an outside buyer or a seller-financed transfer to a group of your employees. Then build your company and your exit plan in a way that will make your endgame a reality.

2. Begin assembling your exit team as soon as you can. I've already addressed the need for a CPA or a CFP® professional with exit-planning experience. You'll also need two more key people:

   › A mergers and acquisitions attorney to handle contracts and stay on top of issues related to regulatory and antitrust law

   › An investment banker or M&A advisor to handle issues related to financing, debt management, stock ownership programs, and other financial matters

Again, as with your CPA and your CFP® professional, you'll want people with plenty of exit experience. It's great if you already have a corporate counsel, but the attorney who sets up your articles of incorporation and advises you about intellectual property protection shouldn't be managing the legal aspects of your exit, because that's likely not his or her area of expertise.

Find people who understand the complexity of the exit-planning process, give them time to learn about you and your business, and stick with them. Remember, you will probably sell a business once in your life, but the key members of your team may have been involved in the sale of dozens of companies. Trust their expertise.

 What do you do when you're less than a year away from your exit date—or you even have an unsolicited offer on the table—and you've done no planning? First, don't panic. Second, drop everything and find your one crucial team member: a CPA or a CFP® professional with extensive exit experience. He or she will advise you on other important first steps and on choosing other professionals for your team.

Did You Know . . . ?

According to the Family Wealth Advisors Council, 90 percent of owners of family-owned businesses want to transfer the business to a family member, but more than 70 percent of those businesses do not survive the transition to the next generation. Sometimes family members just aren't interested in running the company; others lack the skills to keep it profitable, so it fails. This often leads to the founder reassuming control of an ailing business and ultimately losing retirement income. If you want to pass your business to your heirs, start early by finding ways to get them involved in every aspect of the company's operations.

KNOW THE VALUE OF YOUR BUSINESS

It's far better to buy a wonderful company at a fair price than a fair company at a wonderful price. —WARREN BUFFETT

THE FACTS

I regularly hear business owners claim they already know the value of their business. My response is simple: No, you don't. Unless you're in the trenches as a dealmaker, there's no way you can know the value of your company on the open market. Even if you have the financial skill set to conduct an accurate valuation, as the business owner you're not objective. Most owners overestimate the value of their companies, factoring in things such as sweat equity that, while important, don't matter to a buyer.

An accurate valuation of your company will help you do each of the following:

1. *Establish your starting line and the distance to the finish.* Owners need to establish the date they want to exit from the business, the amount of cash they need to extract from the business in order to live the post-work life they want, and who they hope will buy or accept transfer of the business. Without a realistic valuation of the business, you won't have a clue if a buyer is making you a reasonable offer or just yanking your chain.

2. *Test your exit objectives.* One of the first questions you'll need to answer in setting your exit objectives is "How much will I need from the sale of my company to maintain the lifestyle I want in retirement?" The next logical question: "Is the business worth enough (after taxes) to support those needs?" Since the typical owner's business represents about 80 percent of his net worth, answering this question is essential.

Let's assume you decide that your exit objective is to receive $7 million (after taxes) from the transfer of your business interest. You want to exit in three years. An estimate of your company's value will tell you whether the distance between today's value and your finish line is too great to reach in three years. If the growth rate is unrealistic for your business, you must either extend your timeline or lower your financial expectations.

3. *Have a basis for tax planning.* Each exit path has different tax implications. Without appropriate tax planning, taxes can take a huge bite out of your sale proceeds. Given that tax mitigation strategies often take years to implement, it is critical that you start planning well before you exit—and that you use an accurate estimate of value.

4. *Do a litmus test.* Calculate the amount of cash needed to ensure financial security, and subtract from that the value of the business today. This will leave you with a "gap amount"— how much additional value you need to create in order to meet your objectives. With this number in mind, you can start to determine where you should concentrate your time and effort. Instead of growing value for the heck of it, dedication to a goal enables many owners to exit sooner and with more after-tax cash than owners who do no planning. This calculation will also help you know what kind of transfer will best serve your goals. For example, an appropriate business value for a third-party sale may be significantly higher than the value established for a transfer of the same business to key employees, or for a gift of the business to heirs.

5. *Have an objective basis for incentive plans.* Incentive plans are essential for retaining your best people and motivating

them after a sale or transfer. In fact, your sale may be contingent upon key personnel staying; smart buyers know that a company's employees are often its greatest asset. Many owners use incentive programs with a vesting schedule that both motivates and "handcuffs" employees to a company; if a key employee leaves the company, he or she would likely leave a lot of money on the table. The best of these plans, whether cash- or stock-based, are typically built on formulas that link the bonus size to growth in business value.

Before I go any further into this topic, let's clarify some terms that will become important later:

» *Fair market value*—The price a company will likely sell for in a transaction between a hypothetical willing and able buyer and a hypothetical willing and able seller, assuming that both parties have all the relevant facts at hand and that neither coercion nor duress is involved. The cost of getting a fair market valuation from a CPA can range from $5,000 to $20,000, and that scares many entrepreneurs from getting a valuation at all. But while fair market value is important if you're dealing with estate planning, gifting, or divorce, it's not what you need to sell your business to a third party.

» *Open market value*—This is what you need. Open market value is a practical assessment of what your company could fetch on the market today given its strengths and weaknesses, the state of the M&A market, the state of the economy, and other variables. It's a real-world valuation—and getting one costs a great deal less than getting a fair market valuation.

» *EBITDA*—Earnings before interest, taxes, depreciation, and amortization. I've mentioned this already, but it's the most critical number for you to know as you begin contemplating your exit strategy. Typically, the bigger a company is, the greater its EBITDA.

» *Multiple*—A buyer pays for your company's future potential earnings, balanced with the risk that he or she will not get the required rate of return. The sale price that reflects that blend of earnings and risk is stated as a multiple of your EBITDA. Basically, your multiple is a ratio of the total value of your enterprise to your EBITDA. It is very similar to a price-earnings ratio (or "P/E ratio"), which you may be familiar with if you invest in publicly traded stocks.

Based on the market for publicly traded companies, which often sell for ten to twenty times their P/E ratio, many entrepreneurs maintain inflated expectations about the multiple that a buyer will pay for their company. But privately held businesses are riskier—smaller, more vulnerable, tough to market, and with less access to capital—and that brings prices down. Midmarket companies with annual revenues between $5 million and $150 million commonly sell for four to seven times their EBITDA. But companies with less than $5 million in annual revenue typically sell for a multiple of only two or three.

When you sell your company sometime down the line, you may have a certain multiple in mind. Is that number realistic? Do you have the EBITDA to justify it? If not, how much do you need to grow your revenues so you can fetch the kind of offer that will fund your post-work lifestyle? You can't answer any of these questions without knowing the value of your company.

In seeking growth, many owners focus on revenues. However, to improve your company's valuation, consider turning your attention to *earnings* growth—that is, profitability. Your earnings, which can be impacted not only by bringing in more revenue but also by lowering costs, will determine your multiple and your final sale price. When it comes to selling, bigger is always better. If you take two roughly equivalent businesses—each one healthy, sustainable, and efficient—the business with the higher annual earnings will sell for a higher multiple. Why? Because a smaller business is a riskier business. It may not have a diversified customer base or produce enough cash flow to withstand a downturn in its market. Small businesses are more vulnerable to failure than big ones are, so the big ones sell for more. That's the harsh math.

A savvy buyer will look at the risk associated with your company and translate that risk into a percentage figure. That's the rate of return he or she needs to get from the business for the investment to be worth the risk. The higher the rate of return your buyer needs, the lower your multiple will be. It's a simple formula:

The reciprocal of the investor's required rate of return equals your multiple.

Say an investor decides that he or she needs to get a 33 percent rate of return from your business in order to offset the perceived risk. Thirty-three percent is one-third; the reciprocal of that is three. So you'll be offered a multiple of three times EBITDA. But if your business is larger and less risky, an investor might decide he needs only a 20 percent return to justify the risk. Twenty percent is one-fifth; its reciprocal is five. That business will fetch a price of five times EBITDA.

So if growing your business is the smart play, how much do you need to grow? The only way to know that is to find out what your company is worth right now. The "sweet spot"—where buyers begin offering higher multiples to business owners—is $5 million in annual revenue and $500,000 in EBITDA. As soon as a company crosses that threshold, *boom!* It moves from two-to-three-multiple territory into four-to-seven-multiple territory. That can be a difference of a few million dollars in an owner's pocket. So if you're close to that $5 million/$500,000 line, you want to do everything you can to blow past it and make sure that you're seen as a midmarket company, not an owner-operated small business.

There's another good reason to grow beyond that $5 million mark (if you can): less competition for buyers. There are only about 300,000 midmarket companies in the United States with annual revenues ranging from $5 million to $1 billion. But there are more than ten times as many owner-operated small businesses with revenues of less than $5 million. If you're one of them, you have more than three million potential competitors for the attention of the M&A market. Being in the $5 million–plus category makes you part of a more select—and less risky—cohort.

So it makes sense to grow as much as possible before you sell. But how can you know how much to grow earnings—how many people to hire, how many new customers you need, how much additional capital to borrow—unless you know your company's value? You can't. It's impossible to draw a map to the finish line if you don't know where you're starting.

Knowing your company's market value also comes into play when you consider the kind of buyer who is most likely to make you an offer. Buyers fall into two categories:

» *Financial buyers* purchase your company's future profit stream. Their evaluation of your business's worth focuses on the likelihood of those profits flowing in the future. Since buying your company represents a substantial risk, financial buyers will demand a higher return on their investment, and that will drive down your multiple. They are strictly investors;

they bring no synergy to the table. A private equity firm—which will buy a business, grow its value, and then sell it at a substantial profit—is a good example of a financial buyer.

» *Strategic buyers* (which can be competitors, suppliers, or even customers) purchase your company because it adds value to their existing business, perhaps by providing new products to sell or by opening access to a new distribution channel. A strategic buyer determines your company's value by assessing what it might be worth if it were folded into the buyer's enterprise and by taking into account synergies that exist between your business and theirs. Those synergies increase the strategic buyer's calculated earnings potential, which increases your company's valuation.

Knowing your company's value—and knowing whether a business in your industry is more likely to attract a financial or a strategic buyer—will help you gauge just what type of multiple you could expect if you sold today and how much you need to grow in order to get the final sale price you want.

THE SECRET

Get an open market valuation of your company done by a qualified professional. A valuation is not a precise number, but a range that changes over time as your company and industry change and the economy fluctuates. That's why valuing your company is not a

DIY project; you need an expert with the experience and skills to take the changing variables into account.

That does not mean you should go out and spend $10,000 to hire a CPA who's also a Certified Valuation Analyst. You can get an accurate open market valuation by hiring an experienced M&A advisor or CFP® professional for $1,000 to $2,000. You could also turn to your financial advisor, but most advisors are not well schooled in the process of placing a value on a business. Finding an advisor who is proficient in this area can significantly improve your chances of realizing a successful exit.

Placing an open market value on a business is a complex process, but it involves the following basic steps:

1. Cataloging your debt, cash flow, receivables, and return on equity, and assessing them in relation to the standards in your industry.

2. Tracking the trends in your pretax income, revenue, inventory, fixed assets, and receivables.

3. Analyzing a wide range of financial ratios—including debt/equity, cash/debt, and cash flow/revenue—and your cushion in paying the interest on your debt.

4. Using the Standard Industrial Classification (SIC) code for your industry to assess the kinds of values typically attached to your type of business. Valuations are always done on a

per-industry basis, because some sectors are considered more valuable than others. For example, tech companies generally attract higher multiples than manufacturing companies do.

5. Looking at how dependent the company is on any one individual (usually the owner) or customer for its survival. Companies with all their eggs in a single basket have a lower value.

6. Calculating a market value for your business based on the sale of all assets (both physical assets and intangibles such as customer base and goodwill) plus cash, minus liabilities.

Even then, getting a valuation isn't an exact science; there are lots of variables. For instance, if an entrepreneur is using the business to fund his or her lifestyle, it's important to add those lifestyle expenses back to the value of the company. So if a company's EBITDA is $1 million a year but the owner has been using revenues to cover car payments, a country club membership, and personal travel to the tune of $100,000 a year, that $100,000 gets added to EBITDA. Now the company is generating $1.1 million in EBITDA. If the owner sells at a multiple of five, that's an extra $500,000 in his or her pocket.

There's no downside to getting a valuation of your company. It costs a little, but the knowledge you'll gain is worth many times what you'll pay your CFP or M&A advisor.

HOW YOU'LL BENEFIT

The main benefit of getting an accurate valuation is getting a clear picture of the current state of your business. In my experience, most entrepreneurs think they could get more for their company than it's actually worth on the open market. That's understandable; they have an emotional attachment to their company because they've devoted years of their lives to it. But buyers don't care about that; they only care about return on investment. That's why there's usually a substantial gap between what an owner *wants* for the company and what he or she can actually *get* for it.

An accurate valuation closes that gap. Even if you get a rude surprise when the valuation numbers come in, you'll know where you stand. You won't fool yourself into thinking you can sell for $5 million when your company is worth only $500,000. Most important, with the valuation in hand, you'll be able to start making smart, strategic business decisions that will increase the value of your company over time.

Debra Repko, who owns an information systems firm in the Arlington, Virginia, area, provides an example of the power of a good valuation.[4] Debra's company does work for the federal government. She began planning for her exit early, but she assumed that her company was worth much more than it was, in part because it was too dependent on her daily involvement.

Debra's exit goal was to get four to five times EBITDA for

her business. But when an unsolicited offer came in, it was far below that multiple. The prospective buyer felt that the business didn't have the kind of management team in place that would justify a higher valuation. Too many deals and decisions still required Debra's involvement.

Debra was stunned. She passed on the offer and immediately hired a firm to give her an open market valuation of her company. When the number came in quite a bit lower than what she had assumed, she then engaged a consultant to advise her on ways to increase her company's value. The first step: replace herself. Debra hired a chief operating officer and made plans to keep her company for at least three more years so she could grow its value and meet her goals.

"Sometimes when you think you're ready to exit, you're really not," she says. "There are a few things I wish I'd done a few years ago that I'm finally doing today." Wiser after her aborted sale, Debra also pared down her company, eliminating people, projects, and departments that were not profitable. That's another smart step. Buyers love lean, mean businesses with management that has the discipline to control costs and cut what's not working.

Having an up-to-date valuation in your hand also prepares you for situations involving divorce, gifting your business to heirs, or creating an employee stock ownership plan. In these situations, you actually want the stated value of your company to be *lower*. What you're looking for is the "lowest defensible value." In a transfer, that can reduce your tax burden; in a divorce, you lose less if your business is worth less. For these reasons, getting a fair market valuation (despite the higher cost of that service) can be a smart move. To further reduce the company's taxable or legal value, a smart CPA will factor in such things as a business being difficult to sell or a "lack of control" discount. (The latter happens when you gift a small interest in the company to your kids but, because minority owners are unable to make decisions that could have a significant impact on the company, they lack the power to control its direction.)

Getting a professional valuation will also make you aware of the value of shared synergy. I've told you that strategic buyers look for synergies; what you may not know is that those synergies have a specific monetary value. Synergies won't increase your multiple, but the seller of a business will typically see between 10 percent and 50 percent of the value of shared synergies added to its EBITDA.

For example, let's say a strategic buyer in the magazine publishing industry offers $4 million for a digital printing company with an EBITDA of $1 million. That's a multiple of four . . . but wait: Synergies between the two businesses add another $500,000 of earnings to the printing company. The parties agree that the seller will be credited 30 percent of that $500,000—or $150,000—on his EBITDA. Now when the deal closes, instead of getting $4 million, the seller gets $4.6 million. Shared synergy has put an extra $600,000 dollars—four times that additional $150,000—in the seller's bank account. If he hadn't known that he was entitled to the value of those synergies, he might have been snowballed in a sale and lost out on that extra cash.

As you can see, there are many reasons that it makes good sense to get immediate and regular valuations of your company. We recommend updating your valuation every year—typically as part of our clients' annual review process—because it helps us track our progress and gauge how far we are from the finish line. Perhaps the most important reason is the simplest one: If you know what your business is worth, you'll dodge unpleasant surprises. Knowing the value of your business well in advance gives you the opportunity to work on increasing it—and perhaps to accumulate outside investments that will offset a lackluster valuation. I've seen many entrepreneurs sit, silent and stunned, after finding out too late that they were probably never going to be able to retire because their businesses simply didn't have enough value on the open market. Don't be one of them; protect yourself with information. That way, you'll know when a quality offer comes across the table, and if your business isn't worth as much as you thought, you can course-correct while adjusting your personal financial plan.

WHAT TO DO

1. Contact an investment banker or financial advisor today who is well versed in exit planning, and begin a professional valuation of your company. Do it *today*.

2. Set up a schedule to get a new valuation at regular intervals as recommended by your advisory team. I don't suggest getting the fair market value every year; that's simply too expensive. Some business owners never need one—they are typically useful in the courtroom. But as your business evolves, it's vital to know how its value is evolving and the ways that value can turn into money in your pocket.

What will you need to provide for a company valuation? Here's a partial list:

» A detailed description and history of the business

» A detailed description of the company's industry

» A detailed description of the company's customers and over-all market

» A detailed analysis of the key competitors

» A list of assets that will and will not be sold

» Income sources that will be held back, if any

» Quarterly balance sheets for the last three years

» Quarterly income statements for the last three years

» Details on the company's legal and ownership structure

» Information on all liabilities, including payroll, profit sharing, stock options, retirement plans, and bonuses

» Information on agreements with employees and independent contractors

» Information on all company intellectual property—patents, trademarks, etc.

Your valuation and exit-planning advisor(s) can provide you with a comprehensive list. Assembling all these materials may seem like a headache, but it's an important part of a critical process that will reveal things you need to know about your business—and that will help you extract the greatest value from it when the time comes.

Even if you're a year or less away from your exit date, my advice is the same: Get an open market valuation *immediately*. There's not much you can do to improve the value of your company in such a short time, but at least you won't go into the marketplace blind, and you won't turn down a decent purchase offer while holding out for a ridiculous multiple. By spending roughly thirty minutes to complete a questionnaire on our website, www.swpconnect.com, you can obtain a fairly accurate valuation and report for considerably less than $1,000.

Did You Know . . . ?

Some expenses are added back to EBITDA when determining a company's valuation—a process known as *normalizing*. They include the following:

» Excess compensation

» Unearned compensation for family members

» Excessive rent

» Personal travel and entertainment expenses

» Management and directors' fees

» Excessive insurance costs

» Executive compensation that exceeds industry norms

» Unusually large bad debts

» Legal expenses

» Some research and development costs

» Uninsured losses from accidents

» Losses incurred in launching new products or opening new locations

» Cost of accounting audits

» Discontinued customer incentives

» Charitable donations

VALUE IS ABOUT MORE THAN CASH FLOW

There are so many men who can measure costs, and so few who can measure value. —UNKNOWN

THE FACTS

All businesses run on cash, and without enough of it, you won't run for long. Cash flow is the lifeblood of any business. But focusing exclusively on maximizing cash flow can actually hurt your business when it comes time to sell, because doing so can cause you to neglect other facets of your business that may actually have a greater positive impact on your final sale price.

As you execute your exit plan, your focus should be on

increasing the sellable value of your business—its valuation. Most companies are valued as a multiple of their EBITDA:

valuation = EBITDA × multiple

That means there are two ways to increase your business's valuation: One is by increasing cash flow, which will increase EBITDA. The other is by increasing your multiple. The latter is the focus of this section.

Remember, your multiple is a reflection of how risky an investment a buyer perceives your business to be. If a buyer decides—based on analysis of your financials, personnel, operations, and business model—that your business offers a high probability of delivering a desired return on investment and of growing in the future, you'll get a higher multiple. Businesses with greater inherent risks will attract lower multiples. So to increase your multiple—and your valuation—you should be taking steps to reduce the risks associated with your business.

Unfortunately, many of those steps toward risk reduction often have little impact on your quarter-to-quarter cash flow numbers. That's why some entrepreneurs, forever locked into survival mode, ignore them. At best, risk reduction goes in the *I'll get to it eventually* pile. But make no mistake: Over the long term, the factors that impact your multiple can make the difference between walking away with enough money to buy a nice car and walking away with enough to live on for the rest of your life.

Those factors include the following:

» The demand for your type of business within your industry

» The accuracy of your record keeping, quality of your personnel, and condition of your physical facilities and equipment

» The health of your chief competitors

» Your business's recent profit history

» General economic conditions, both nationally and in your region

» Potential synergies between your company and others

» Your preferred terms for selling your business

» The legal structure of your company and the nature of existing employee, vendor, or customer contracts

Some of the factors that will most profoundly impact your company's value, however, relate to *revenue* and *expenses*. All revenues are not created equal. The *type* of revenue that provides most of your company's income will have as much to do with the kind of multiple a buyer will offer as the amount of revenue. Because buyers are always seeking to minimize risk, *recurring* revenues will attract higher multiples than sporadic or *nonrecurring* revenues will. Recurring revenues are predictable and considered likely to continue into the future. Examples include the following:

» Subscriptions (e.g., annual or monthly access fees for magazines or newspapers)

» Monthly fees for service (e.g., mobile phone contracts)

» Retainer fees (e.g., standard, recurring fees paid to a consultant or advertising agency)

» Membership fees (e.g., auto-renewing fees for warehouse stores or health clubs)

» Renewing service contracts (e.g., tech support packages or car warranties)

» Annual licenses (e.g., rights fees for software or media)

As you can imagine, automatically renewing revenues that recur based on contractual agreements are the cream of the crop, being the closest most businesses will get to guaranteed, ongoing cash flow. Recurring revenues reduce risk by acting as a buffer against market volatility, which can cripple a small company that lacks a dependable source of ongoing revenue. Because of this, businesses with a substantial stream of recurring revenues are valued more highly than businesses that depend primarily on nonrecurring revenues.

Nonrecurring revenue sources include both sales of expensive products that customers don't repurchase regularly and sales that require costly, time-consuming processes that are not easily replicated. Because they don't produce dependable streams of income, these revenue sources increase a company's volatility and thus a buyer's risk.

The way you treat expenses also impacts your company's

value. One of the most common problems I see is business owners who don't reveal the lifestyle expenses that they pay for with revenues from the company. It's important to disclose those kinds of personal expenses so that overall expenses can be normalized. There's nothing wrong with using company revenues to pay for laptop computers, travel, or your sailboat; it's your company and your money. But those expenses should not reduce the sellable value of your business.

Bottom line: Cash flow will always be essential in determining the value of your business. However, it's more important that buyers see your business as a *quality* business.

THE SECRET

With all that talk about revenues in mind, it's time to stop focusing your time and attention exclusively on strategies designed to increase cash flow. *Cash flow remains important, but in exit planning it's just as important to invest your energies in implementing the "value drivers" that can reduce risk, position your company as a quality business worth investing in, and ultimately increase the multiple you command.*

What are value drivers? They are those characteristics of a business that either reduce the risk associated with owning the business or enhance the prospect that the business will grow significantly in the future.

The reason a buyer is willing to pay a premium price for a business centers on his or her perception of risk and return. If characteristics that reduce risk and improve return are present, a buyer will pay top dollar in the form of a higher multiple. Buyers will compare the risk and return of buying your business to the risk and return involved in alternative investment opportunities. By lowering risk and upping potential return, value drivers improve your odds of getting an offer at the multiple you want.

There are plenty of value drivers, but the following ones are common to virtually every business, regardless of industry:

» *A diverse customer base.* Smart buyers want to know that your company is not dependent on a small number of key customers for most of its income. If 80 percent of your revenue comes from just two key customers, what happens if one of them suddenly goes belly up? A business that could see half its annual revenues disappear with a single phone call is not a business that many buyers would consider worth a large multiple.

The ideal approach is something commonly called the "Switzerland Structure." In this business model, you're customer neutral, just as Switzerland is politically neutral. Your company has a broad, diverse base of established customers (many that have been with you for years), none of which represents more than a small percentage of your total revenue. This way, losing any one of those customers isn't a fatal blow.

» *Stable, predictable cash flow.* Cash is king. Every small business owner knows that cash flow determines whether a company survives or falls by the wayside. Prospective buyers know this too, and they will pay higher multiples for a company whose cash flow trajectory is steadily rising.

Take proactive steps to improve cash flow, and you will increase your chances of finding a top-quality buyer. Weed out inefficiencies in your operations, and reduce costs. Find ways to increase employee productivity. Reevaluate your return on investment in such areas as advertising and marketing. Stop using company revenues to pay your personal expenses. Look for ways to save money on your employee benefits, especially with the new healthcare exchanges opening in many states. Put off or cancel large capital expenditures that don't directly increase capacity. Buyers love lean, well-run businesses that spend what they must to compete and deliver excellence—but don't *overspend.*

» *Strong, independent management.* Note the word *independent.* One of the most common mistakes owners make is building a team of experienced, committed managers . . . and then not letting them do their jobs. A management team is often the key asset purchased in a deal; buyers are willing to pay more for a strong management team with a solid track record of making quality decisions. A mollycoddled management team that has never been given the power to execute high-level decisions will reduce the value of that asset. A business that is completely dependent on its founder for decision making is a business with little sellable value.

Buyers crave stability. If the current owner makes all the decisions, it will be unclear whether the management team has the skill set required to make the necessary decisions to ensure ongoing profitability of the company after the owner's departure. So boosting market value means removing yourself from day-to-day operations, building a management team that includes people with a variety of skills, and putting in place incentives that keep those valuable people with the business after it sells. Consider establishing a compensation system that rewards key employees with cash or stock when the company meets or exceeds performance expectations. Making some of that incentive compensation deferred or subject to vesting also helps keep great managers around longer.

» *A clear, comprehensive "owner's manual."* Does your business have written processes and systems in place? Could a buyer come in tomorrow, read those documents, and use them to keep the business running profitably? If the answer is no, you have a problem.

Document everything: sales processes, HR policies, quality control methodology, your IT systems, ways of getting and following up on leads, tips for maintaining relationships with current customers—everything you do in order to generate consistent revenues and keep your customers satisfied. Create printed and electronic documents that can serve as a buyer's how-to guide. Your goal should be to give a buyer confidence that a post-sale transition will be smooth and disruptions minimal.

» *Solid financials.* Questionable financial records spell doom for a sale. Since any buyer will do his or her due diligence and review your books, smart owners turn this process into an asset by maintaining clean, meticulously kept financials. The best way to do this is to have your financial statements prepared by a qualified CPA and regularly audited by an independent accounting firm. Audits are the cost of doing business the right way and a hallmark of a quality company.

» *Proper legal structure.* When you incorporate, your new corporation will be a "C" corporation (under subchapter C of the tax code) unless you file for "S" status. S and C corporations both enjoy limited liability, which is the main reason that owners incorporate their small businesses. The big difference between the two comes in tax liability. Like LLCs, companies that operate as S corporations are taxed as a pass-through entity, meaning the income of the business is treated as the income of the owners and is taxed only once. C corporations pay taxes twice—the corporation pays tax on its net income, and then the shareholders pay tax on distributions. Double taxation can have a chilling effect on a buyer. Switching from a C corporation to an S is complex, however, so get sound legal advice *before* you incorporate, if possible.

» *A path to growth in a growing industry*. Buyers offer higher multiples for companies that have a realistic growth strategy. Your job is to communicate the reasons that cash flow will increase and the business will grow after the deal closes. Reasons could include the development of new products; increased demand for your products or services because of changes in the economy; expansion into new markets; or future acquisitions. Have facts and figures ready to show buyers in detail why your business is poised to thrive.

HOW YOU'LL BENEFIT

Quite simply, by focusing on the value drivers specific to your business, you'll create a higher-quality company with a better chance of attracting a higher multiple from a buyer. As an example, consider Cory Janssen, cofounder of financial information website Investopedia and of Divestopedia, an online information center for business owners seeking to sell their companies. When Cory and his wife founded Investopedia in 1999, he was doing all the selling and his wife was doing the books. That went on through 2002, when the company had grown to nearly thirty employees. At that point, Cory realized that they could no longer act like a mom-and-pop business.

"From 2004 through 2007, we focused on destroying our own jobs and putting processes in place," he says. "We delegated everything possible. We started working on the business instead of in the business. We hired an exit planner to give us an outside look at things. We also hired people who were smarter than we were."

Cory had the common sense to know that he could sell only so much online advertising while sitting a thousand miles away from the advertising centers of New York, Chicago, and Los Angeles. He and his wife had built a thriving business without knowing what they were doing, but taking it to the next level meant building a sales force. So that's what he did.

Of course, finding the right people wasn't easy. Cory explains:

> What they don't tell you in the entrepreneur books is how to hire great people, motivate them, and keep them around. The reality is, a lot of the people with the brains and drive and talent have already started their own businesses. We'd hire someone, it wouldn't work, and we'd ask ourselves if it was the process or the person. We'd decide it was the person, and we'd bring in a new person.

Eventually you get the right person, and then you go to work perfecting the process. You keep on trying to improve incrementally. The ability to consistently find, motivate, and retain brilliant people might be what makes a Bill Gates.[5]

Cory isn't Bill Gates, but his efforts to add value certainly paid off: In 2007, Forbes Media LLC bought Investopedia for an undisclosed amount.

WHAT TO DO

You don't have to tackle every item on the value drivers list today. But if you are two to five years away from your desired exit date, then you should begin implementing some key value drivers right away.

1. A terrific way to get guidance in doing this is to join a CEO peer group like Young Presidents' Organization (YPO), Entrepreneurs' Organization (EO), or Vistage. These organizations will provide you with an advisory board of your peers who are interested in helping you improve your business. You will benefit from the experience of other entrepreneurs who have already engaged in the process you're just starting.

2. Think like Cory Janssen and start making some of the changes that he and his partners made. Start by restructuring your business so it can operate independently of you, the founder and owner. This is one of the best ways you can add value (and I'll talk a lot more about this in the next section). Apart from making the business less dependent on your involvement in every decision, you'll also spend less time working on tasks below your pay grade. If you're the brains of the outfit, you shouldn't be doing the books, writing the press releases, or reviewing the contracts. While some entrepreneurs believe that handling those tasks is saving them money, smart entrepreneurs know how substantial the opportunity cost is. Outsource or delegate everything you can, and free yourself to work on things that add substantial value.

3. Start putting together your top-flight management team. These should be people with the skills and talents to take over the operation of your business when you eventually sell. Set up programs that align these people's interests with the company's interests—bonuses, profit sharing, paid leave, and the like.

4. Audit your processes for inefficiencies and wasteful spending. This is another immediate step you can take to create value. Look ruthlessly at such things as travel, benefits, training, and gifts, and figure out where you can trim spending

without damaging productivity or morale. For example, one company spent $100,000 a year giving its employees free turkeys at Thanksgiving and Christmas that almost nobody wanted. After they did an audit and found out most people were donating the turkeys, the company simply donated its own turkeys, took a charitable deduction, and threw its employees a terrific holiday party that cost only $10,000. The net savings to the company was about $90,000 a year. That adds up.

5. Finally, do an inventory of your customers. How stable are they? Are you too dependent on a few "sugar daddies"? How vulnerable are your key customers to failure or buyout, and what would happen if you lost them tomorrow? Ask yourself the tough questions, and use the answers to help you develop strategies for growing the diversity and stability of your customer base.

Eventually, try to take decisive action on all the value drivers supporting your company. If you don't think you have time, think about this: In four years, Cory Janssen took steps that made tiny startup Investopedia valuable enough that Forbes bought it. It can be done. You can do it.

Make sure you document all your systems and procedures so a buyer has a clear, comprehensive how-to manual for running the company after your exit. If you already have your processes and systems documented, get them updated. Markets, technology, and people change, and your company's procedural documents need to change with them. Create a step-by-step owner's manual for every part of your business, no matter how small.

Did You Know . . . ?

Another good reason for maintaining a stable management team is to demonstrate a healthy corporate culture. Corporate culture matters to buyers because employee turnover is expensive, and a strong culture reduces turnover. If your exit strategy is short-term, consider implementing programs to improve employee morale. These can include informal, social get-togethers; flexible work hours; written statements of appreciation for good work; ample opportunities for promotion; challenging assignments; company-sponsored continuing education; and periodic surveys to measure job satisfaction and allow employees to express their concerns.

MAKE YOURSELF EXPENDABLE

The best executive is the one who has sense enough to pick good men to do what he wants done, and self-restraint enough to keep from meddling with them while they do it. —**THEODORE ROOSEVELT**

THE FACTS

One of the most common barriers to sellability, especially for small businesses with less than $5 million in revenues, is owner over-involvement. Too many small business owners are simply so involved in every aspect of the day-to-day operations of their companies that they frighten off potential buyers. The smaller the business, the more likely it becomes that the owner and founder is the source of most or all of the key relationships and revenue-producing activities that keep the business afloat. If the owner left on Thursday, by Monday the business would be on the verge of collapse.

Not long ago, I met with a gentleman who owned an apparel company doing about $10 million in annual revenues. He told me he was thinking about selling in a few years, and I asked him, "How involved are you with day-to-day operations?" Turns out, he was still in charge of the five biggest customer accounts, representing 35 percent of his company's total revenue. I told him that if he wanted to sell for the highest possible value, he had to hand off those accounts to someone else.

Allowing your company to become too dependent on your presence is completely understandable. Starting a company is an intense, emotional experience in which entrepreneurs become personally invested. They take pride in being the source of the activities that make the business run. The company becomes, in essence, their "baby." They can't imagine surrendering control to anyone else, even someone with a stronger business background. Sure, there's an element of control in this; most successful entrepreneurs have a bit of the control freak in them. But it's also a practical matter. If you've run your business for ten years, you've built up relationships of trust with your key customers and vendors. You can't just transfer that trust to some anonymous management team.

Or can you? More to the point, should you?

The short answer is yes. If you think of your business as your child, then think about this: Every parent's job is to raise children who, one day, can go off into the world on their own and be successful while living independent lives. The alternative is having your forty-five-year-old unemployed "kid" living in your basement. Your job as an entrepreneur is to "raise" a business that can run independently of you.

Having a business that cannot operate independently of its owner is a huge handicap in the search for a solid purchase offer. If you are not only the company CEO but also the chief salesperson and sole decision maker, then you *are* the company. And since remaining on board as a key employee—virtually selling yourself along with your business—sort of defeats the purpose of an exit plan, the business will have little or no value without you. That presents a potentially deal-killing obstacle for a buyer. If your company lurches to a halt when you're not there to make every decision, you're creating additional risk that will, at best, depress your multiple and, at worst, chase away qualified buyers.

Here's how having a business that's too dependent on you can kill your open market value:

1. *You're the sole source of the processes, systems, and trade secrets that have made your company successful.* If you leave without spending enough time and energy to share this profound

understanding with the right people, the company probably will collapse.

2. *Your customers and vendors trust you and identify with you—and no one else.* In their minds, their relationship is with *you,* not your company. It will be extremely challenging—and potentially impossible—for the new owners to recapture that trust, no matter how skilled and well-meaning they are. It's likely that once you've moved on, so will those customers and vendors.

3. *You have not given your subordinates the opportunity to run their segments of the company autonomously.* Because of this, your employees may not have developed as self-starters or good decision makers. That can cripple the company after you're gone.

4. *You suffer from "entrepreneuritis" and have infected your whole company.* Many entrepreneurs thrive on chaos, challenge, long hours, and problem solving. A business that runs too smoothly isn't stimulating, so they purposefully run some aspects of the company by the seat of their pants, even if they've been in business for twenty years. This may give you an adrenaline rush, but the result is a company with serious inefficiencies and procedural flaws.

5. *You're elbow-deep in your business, and a buyer will be saddled with your workload.* If you're working day and night

in your business, it's not likely to be self-sustaining—it's a sixty-hour-per-week job for anyone who runs it. No buyer is going to spend a few million dollars to buy himself a job with *built-in, unpaid overtime.*

6. *You're wasting your time and skills on menial work that can be done by somebody else.* You're the big thinker, the industry expert. Are you best serving your company and employees by changing toner cartridges and doing payroll? Of course not. At some point, you should be outsourcing most of your former duties so you can focus on developing strategy, opening new markets, and other areas in which you can actually create substantial additional value for your business.

Take an honest look at your relationship to the business. Are you so deeply involved in every part of your company's operations that you're a threat to its sellability? There's a simple test: Ask yourself when you last took a vacation. According to a 2012 survey conducted by Manta, the online business information network, about 50 percent of small business owners do not take any vacation time.[6] And 70 percent of the owners who do manage to get away tether themselves to their companies via smartphones and tablets. It's all part of a trend: According to the American Express OPEN Small Business Vacation Monitor, business owner getaways have been on the decline since 2006.[7]

I'm going to go out on a limb and state flat out that if you can't find a way to take two weeks off from running your business (and I'm talking about being completely out of touch, not taking meetings via Skype from your beach lounger), you don't have a business that can be sold on the open market. That leads directly to Tepper's Inverse Law of Owner Involvement:

> **The fewer hours you spend working at your company, the more valuable it will be to a buyer on the open market.**

That's a bit of an oversimplification, but the principle is sound. If you're able to take long vacations and delegate most of your responsibilities to subordinates with no falloff in productivity or profits, it's likely that you have clean, effective processes and smart, dedicated people who will do a great job running the business even after you depart. That kind of continuity is critical for a buyer. Anyone who invests in your company needs to be confident that after the sale closes and the champagne toasts are over, there won't be a "hangover" period during which morale slumps, sales drop, and revenue craters.

The larger your company grows, the less you should be directly involved in the day-to-day mechanics of keeping the lights on and the cash flowing. You should start governing, not managing. You should start building the company's brand, one that's independent of yourself. You are not one of the company's sellable assets.

It is not difficult to spot the danger signs that your business is too dependent on you:

» *You don't take vacations.* Or if you do, you're always checking in. If the business can't survive without you for a week, how will it stay afloat when you're gone for good?

» *You're on a first-name basis with all your customers.* If every relationship that is important to the company is a personal relationship between you and that particular customer, then detaching yourself without damaging revenues is impossible.

» *You sign all the checks.* If you haven't hired someone whom you can trust to pay the bills and take better care of your money than you do, then you're probably holding the reins of your company too tightly.

» *Processes and procedures exist only in your head.* You know exactly how to follow up with key prospects and turn them into customers . . . but nobody else does, because you haven't written anything down.

» *You get sucked into debates about insignificant things.* Issues that are less than mission critical, from office furniture choices to break-room policies, should be handled by management-level employees, not the head of the company.

» *You try to control every last detail.* If you spend all your time micromanaging day-to-day affairs, you have no time left for big-picture planning.

» *You rarely call in sick.* If no one in your company has the experience, training, and personal skills to take over when you're out for a day, what would happen in the event you were to suddenly leave, die, or become disabled?

» *You hire smart people, then underutilize them.* Intending to delegate many of your responsibilities to your best and brightest isn't enough—you have to actually do it.

» *The business is not scalable.* If many of your business processes are unnecessarily labor-intensive and very little is automated, your company is probably too dependent on you to survive without you.

As John Warrillow says in *Built to Sell,* if customers are constantly asking for you and insisting on doing business only with you, and if you're personally involved in serving those customers, you probably have a business that is not sellable. In fact, I would go so far as to say that a small business with an obsessively hands-on owner not only has no chance of growing to become a mid-market company but also has half the chance of finding a buyer.

THE SECRET

Take concrete steps to become less involved in the daily operations of your business. Embrace what Josh Patrick, founder and principal at Stage 2 Planning Partners, calls "passive ownership."[8] The object is to make yourself expendable so the profit-generating activities that now depend on you can be outsourced to others. Your goal should be to become anonymous, no longer the face of the company.

First, stop thinking like an entrepreneur. In the beginning, owning your company may have been more like a lifestyle and even an adrenaline rush, but it's not anymore. Now, it's a set of systems, processes, and people designed to deliver a product or service and make money. That's how any buyer will view it, and you must start doing the same. If you've resisted automating some processes or hiring people to take over certain tasks because you still love the feeling of being a bootstrapper and entrepreneur, it's time to start thinking of yourself as a CEO instead.

Next, take an inventory of all the things you do in your business, from turning on the lights to changing the coffee filters to locking up at the end of the day. Is it a long list? That's a problem. You might think you're holding on to a bunch of menial tasks because you want to make sure everything gets done right or want to show your employees that you're still "one of the guys." Maybe you feel that each of those tasks takes only a few minutes, and therefore you are reluctant to delegate them. However, it's likely that you complete hundreds of those small tasks each week, which can occupy a lot of your time. Without realizing it, you could be consuming dozens of hours each month on nonsense, when you could be spending that time growing large-scale market opportunities. Doing too much of the minor stuff kills your capacity to do the most important work any business owner can do: growing the business.

In order to increase your company's open market value and appeal to a buyer, you've got to free up capacity by letting go of daily operations. You should be engaging in only the kinds of activities a CEO would engage in. Would the CEO of a publicly traded corporation empty the office trashcans or pick up the cake for an employee birthday party? Of course not. Once you have created that list of your activities, start crossing out those that could be delegated to someone else—either a current employee or a new hire. Cross out about 80 percent of the day-to-day activities that consume your time right now.

Of all the activities you clear from your plate, the most important is removing yourself from customer relationships. This is difficult but necessary. You may have built your company from nothing on the strength of a handful of key relationships that you've spent twenty years nurturing. But if you haven't made the effort to expand that relationship to include your employees, those customers probably believe the only way they can do business with your company is by doing business with you. When you leave, their business will leave.

No buyer will purchase a company in such a vulnerable state. Your mission is to take yourself out of the sales and customer service equation. Train your best people to service those key customers. Broker new, trusting relationships between your key customers and your sales and service reps. Then get out of the way.

When you've done these things, you can focus on *governing* your business, not managing it. Keep your eyes on the big picture: brand development, expansion, lobbying, developing new products, key acquisitions, and so on. Those 30,000-foot-level activities will add tremendous long-term value to your company, but you won't have time to address them if you're inventorying the copier paper.

HOW YOU'LL BENEFIT

Kurt Noer, founder and CEO of Customer Magnetism, launched his company in 2000 as a search engine optimization business. Since then it's grown into a full-service Internet marketing agency offering pay-per-click advertising, email marketing, web design, and social media strategy.

Not long ago, Kurt did something that would turn many business owners pale: He took four months off to work on a DIY home project. To his delight, the business ran perfectly without him. That suggests to me that he has been successful in delegating important tasks to the people he's chosen to run the business—and that when the time comes for Kurt to sell, he'll be able to get a premium multiple. He's built a profit-generating system, not a job. "Even now, I'm really just working on additional ways to improve the company further," Kurt says. "I really don't need to be here anymore."[9]

That's one of the major benefits of stepping away from daily management: more free time. If you've spent every waking hour of the past few years working to keep your company alive, you could probably use some time off—after all, isn't that part of the reason you're creating an exit strategy? But the greatest benefit is the increase in both the sellability and the value of your company. By taking yourself out of daily operations and depending on the skills and ideas of your managers, you demonstrate to a buyer that those managers have the ability to run—and grow—the business after you're gone. Remember, a buyer will view your company as a machine designed to deliver value and create profit, and your people are the key parts in that machine.

Of course, the changes that took Customer Magnetism from one-man show to award-winning, internationally recognized agency didn't happen on their own or overnight. They required planning. As Kurt says:

> Follow the *E-Myth Revisited* concept of working *on* your business instead of *in* your business, so you can build a company that flourishes without you instead of a business that only works because of you. Hire people who are smarter than you. And do lots of delegating. It can be frustrating to release decisions to a newly promoted president, because he will absolutely do some things differently than you. Your job is to steer [your employees]

the best you can and then let them make a few mistakes along the way. With my people, for everything they did that was wrong, they made two or three decisions that were brilliant.

As Kurt points out, when you're micromanaging everything, it's like you're stuck in one of those nine-foot-tall European hedge mazes. You can't see where you're going, and you certainly can't see what your options are. But when you let go of the daily to-do list, you become the guy climbing a tree to get a peek from above the maze. Looking down, you can see the whole thing, including the dead ends and the paths that lead you to your goal.

Having a clearer big-picture perspective, making more time to work on initiatives that grow revenue and profits, and building a seasoned team of people who can run things for you so you're only at the office five hours a week—that's how you breed a business that will sell for a high multiple.

WHAT TO DO

Over and over again, the toughest hurdle for entrepreneurs to clear is surrendering control of daily operations. They're just not comfortable with it. My advice: Start delegating some of your duties right away. Don't wait to hire people to fill new management positions; that can become an excuse for procrastination. Choose your best and brightest, promote them or increase their compensation if it's appropriate, and assign them some of the tasks that you struggle with. Over time, move on to handing over the tasks you do well and enjoy. The more you delegate, the more sellable your company will become.

Other specific steps you can take in the next twelve to twenty-four months include the following:

1. *Create a "user's manual" of written, replicable procedures that anyone can use to put your company on autopilot.* Think of this as a handbook that will allow a buyer to sit in your chair and immediately start generating cash flow. It should include your processes for such things as fulfilling orders, hiring and training new personnel, handling customer complaints, communicating with new sales prospects, backing up critical data, and ensuring facility security.

2. *Develop a training program to teach your people how to run your business.* More than one person should be able to manage the customer e-newsletter, make delivery schedules, and approve contracts. Your goal: to never have to explain to someone how to handle a routine business task. Training takes those activities off your plate completely.

3. *Hire people to run key areas of your company such as operations, marketing, and technology.* Make sure those people are smarter than you, and make sure they will stay with the company. Some buyers will insist that essential employees remain

with the company for a certain period; adding noncompete agreements to employment contracts can help ensure this outcome. Give key top people incentives to stick around, such as a nonqualified deferred compensation plan with a vesting schedule.

4. *Avoid making any of your new hires irreplaceable.* There should be no single person without whom your business can't function.

5. *Don't fall into the trap of hiring an assistant as a substitute for giving up most of your responsibilities.* All you'll get is someone else you have to manage, and you already don't have the time to do the things your business needs you to do. Delegate your tasks completely—don't even monitor their execution. Choose people you trust to do the job . . . and then trust them to do the job.

6. *Establish reporting systems that automatically monitor sales activity, quality control, and other critical areas.* Doing this puts the business, not you, in control of ensuring that goals are met.

7. *Remove yourself from your company's brand.* If your business is named after you, rename it. If you have been front and center in your marketing campaigns and media coverage, step out of the spotlight. You are not a sellable commodity; you can't afford to have your company bound up with your personal

identity. From new visual branding to hiring a company spokesperson to appear in commercials, do everything you can to distance yourself from the company you've built. It might hurt, but—like ripping off a Band-Aid—if it has to be done, do it all at once and all the way.

8. *Take vacations—and document them.* This is a terrific way to show that the business can operate well in your absence. At least once a year, take a two-week vacation during which you don't check in. While you're away, have someone in operations document sales, productivity, and any problems. If you've built a self-sustaining business, you shouldn't see any falloff in efficiency or performance. If you do see problems, then you'll know you have work to do. Eventually, you can use these vacation reports to show a buyer how independent your business is.

Bottom line: The more smoothly and profitably your business runs without your daily, hands-on involvement, the more valuable the business you've built. Letting go might be a blow to your ego, but you should be proud of building an independent company that can thrive without you. That's an accomplishment.

 If you're almost out of time, hire a COO and walk away. The most valuable thing you can do to wean your company off your involvement is to install a chief operating officer as soon as possible. Find someone brilliant whose ideas differ from yours. Train him or her in every aspect of your company's operations, and then turn the new boss loose—and stay out of the way. You're sure the business is sound—it can stay afloat without you at the helm, right? Now prove it.

Did You Know . . . ?

Taking a vacation could actually make you a better business owner. According to a study by American Express, more than one-third of small business owners say their best ideas—including the ideas that help their businesses grow—come while they are taking a well-deserved break, not when they're at the office. In fact, according to a study by the *National Leisure Travel Monitor,* the average person exhibits a 25 percent increase in work performance after returning from a vacation.[10]

PART II

MONETIZING

VALUE

SELLING IS YOUR BEST EXIT OPTION

Few men of action have been able to make
a graceful exit at the appropriate time.
—MALCOLM MUGGERIDGE, AUTHOR AND SATIRIST

THE FACTS

Some entrepreneurs dream about handing over their business to their children or selling it to a group of loyal, dedicated employees. In their minds, their children are industrious and business savvy, with the same passion for running the company these founders had when they started it. In the dream, the employees are dedicated and shrewd, with the financial resources to make the company a success long after the founder departs.

Unfortunately, the reality is that the children of business owners often lack the skills to run the business or the desire to work long hours to make it thrive. As for employee groups, they might love the company as much as you do, but they frequently come up short in the money department (as do the children). That can lead to seller financing, which makes it nearly impossible for you to extract anything close to full value from what you've built.

Neither passing your business to your heirs nor selling it to your employees is the optimal exit path for the great majority of entrepreneurs. If your goal is to leave your company with the financial resources and freedom you need to live the post-work life you have planned on, a sale to a third party—otherwise known as an *external transfer*—is almost always your best option.

The main reason for this is the most obvious one: Selling to an outside buyer gives you the best chance to make the most money from the business you've spent a lifetime building. For many entrepreneurs, the sale of their company is their primary source of retirement income—and if they have not contributed to a personal 401(k) plan, a Simplified Employee Pension (SEP), or another tax-deferred retirement account, it may be their *only* source of retirement income. Often a sale to employees or family members will fetch a lower price than a sale on the open market to a strategic or financial buyer. A gift to one's heirs, of course, provides the owner with no income at all. If you're ready to retire and you do not have a nest egg of other assets, selling to a third party could be your only realistic option.

In most cases, you will realize the highest sale price and net the most money at closing from a sale to a strategic buyer. Remember, a strategic buyer buys a company because it complements his or her existing company—and increases its value—in some way. A good example of a strategic buyer would be a large cable company that buys a smaller, regional cable provider because the acquisition opens up new territories where the large company currently has no customers. Strategic buyers may be willing to pay a higher price for your company if there are strong synergies between your business and theirs: complementary product lines, penetration into additional markets, employee overlap, or proprietary technology, to name a few.

If a strategic buyer is not available, private equity firms are another attractive option. Though they are financial buyers looking to pick up your company merely for its cash flow, they have money to spend: According to the December 2012 *Middle Market M&A News* report from Deloitte Corporate Finance, private equity buyout funds had over $430 billion of uninvested capital in the third quarter of 2012, with multiples paid for midmarket companies increasing to their highest levels since 2005.[11]

The financial return aside, an external transfer may be your simplest exit option. Sales to family or employees can require complicated seller financing agreements, along with that lurking risk that you may have to reassume control of the company if your buyers don't make their payments. While employee stock ownership plans (ESOPs) may be a viable option, they can be costly to set up (I will explain more about these a little later). Even gifting requires some complex tax planning and time. If you're looking for a clean exit, sell to a strategic or financial buyer.

Of course, your family members might have no interest in taking over your company (a common situation), and your top managers might have neither the desire nor the skills to run it profitably. If that's the case, a sale to an outside buyer may be not just your simplest option but your only option. This is a great reason to make sure you've implemented my first four secrets. If you have a sound exit plan, controlled costs, growing profits, and minimal hands-on involvement, you're ready to look at selling.

THE SECRET

External transfers offer business owners the greatest potential for monetizing the value they've created over years of building their businesses. But to extract the greatest financial benefit from your exit, you must understand how an external transfer comes together and progresses. Since very few owners of midmarket businesses have any M&A experience, it's worth going into detail here on the process you'll undergo when you actually sell your company. What happens and in what order? How does it all come together?

I'll answer those questions with the help of Dan Weinmann, senior vice president of EdgePoint Capital Advisors in Beachwood, Ohio. Dan is an investment banker with years of experience in selling midmarket businesses with between $5 million and $100 million in annual revenue. He makes an important point about using an investment banker to sell your company:

> Don't just use your accountant. Your CPA will charge you hourly to introduce you to other customers. That's brokering, not making a market. A business broker might put something on a website and wait for people to see it. The trouble with that is, it puts the buyer in charge. An investment banker will take you through a "controlled auction" process instead. That puts the seller in charge, and that's going to get you more money at the end of the day.

To demystify things, Dan and I have mapped out the sale process step by step. Here's what typically happens when you decide to sell your company:

1. You will meet with investment bankers, who will give you their pitch. They'll probably give you an open market valuation of your company and suggest likely buyer groups. They might also suggest strategies such as splitting up a company with two very different product lines that might not be sellable to a single buyer.

2. Your chosen investment banker (IB) will give you an engagement letter, which will include a retainer fee equal to about 10 percent of the firm's expected commission on the sale of your company. So if the banking firm expects to earn about $250,000 from the sale, your retainer will be $25,000, which will be deducted from the final commission. When you sign the letter, you will have your investment banker.

3. The IB will tour your facilities and interview you for at least half a day and perhaps as much as two days. He or she will ask every conceivable question about your company: how it started, who your key customers are, the trends within your industry, who your key managers are, and so on.

4. Using this information, the IB will produce an operation memorandum or confidential information memorandum (CIM). This is the "book" on your company, including detailed financials, operational processes, and so on. Running fifty to sixty pages, this guide will give prospective buyers everything they need to know in order to make a buying decision.

5. Once you approve your "book," your IB will give you a list of potential buyers. These will mostly be private equity groups and strategic companies in your industry. Depending on the size of your company, there might be a few hundred potential buyers or just a few dozen. Companies typically will not purchase a business whose revenues represent less than 5

percent of the purchasing company's revenues; the transaction simply consumes too much money and time for such a small bump in revenue. So if your business does $3 million in revenues, you're not likely to attract much interest from companies larger than $60 million.

Your IB will also filter potential buyers by their deal preferences. For instance, some buyers look for deals with a lot of assets, while others want to keep the acquired assets light.

Together, you and your IB will create a final list of potential buyers—usually from fifty to three hundred names in length—and start making calls. "I always call instead of sending letters," says Dan. "Letters can be ignored, but I call until I talk to someone."

6. Your IB will tell each prospective buyer that a business in your industry is available and will ask whether this business fits the prospect's strategy. The banker will also inquire whether the prospect has done acquisitions before.

7. If the prospect is interested, the IB will send a teaser or an executive summary. This doesn't identify your company, but it identifies your industry, some details about the company, and your financials (both revenue and EBITDA).

8. If the prospective buyer expresses interest in learning more, the IB sends a confidentiality agreement. This is one of the

big differences between working with an investment banker and a business broker. Many brokers will send confidentiality agreements with the client's name on the cover—but of course, disclosing the name of the company prior to having a signed confidentiality agreement isn't very confidential. That opens up the seller to all sorts of abuse in the market. Leaked news about a company being for sale can jeopardize relationships with employees, customers, vendors, and competitors. If a leaked sale doesn't end up happening, the company can be viewed all of a sudden as "tainted goods."

With an IB, the prospect doesn't learn the identity of the selling company until they sign the agreement. Notice that this process can produce several interested prospective buyers, none of whom know the selling company and none of whom have been given a price. This controlled auction format puts you in command of the engagement and lets you drive up the price.

9. Once the prospect signs the confidentiality agreement, your IB will send the CIM, the "book" on your business. The prospective buyer will get two or three weeks to review the information and submit an offer.

10. After the review period, your IB will ask the prospect for an indication of interest, or IOI. This is usually a one-page letter

in which the prospective buyer makes an offer based on its own valuation of your business and suggests other possible aspects of a deal, such as terms or conditions. This is where a good IB separates the players from the onlookers. "At this stage we're gauging interest," says Dan. "If someone isn't willing to put their thoughts into a one-page letter, they're not going to put time into a fifty-page purchase agreement."

11. Your IB will choose the prospects that are the best qualified and make the best offers, show you their IOIs, and ask which ones you want to meet with. The banker will then invite people from those companies to a meeting.

12. Now comes the management presentation. At each company's meeting you and your key managers will present a history of the company, talk about what makes it different, talk about its growth trends, explain the industry, and defend the information in the "book." This is when the buyer decides if the company is a good fit and if the two parties can be partners. These meetings typically last four to five hours each. The parties that have the best personal chemistry are the most likely to wind up doing a deal, because they tend to have similar values and care about similar things.

13. After the management presentations, your IB will ask you to pick one prospective buyer to negotiate with. After you

decide, the banker will send a letter of intent. This is a non-binding but formal document that asks the prospect to respond with a specific bid on the company and gives the prospect a ninety-day exclusivity window to close the transaction. But a smart IB will also use this time to drive up the price as much as possible. "I don't go out with a price," says Dan. "I ask for a blind bid. I also tell the prospect that if they don't close the transaction during the exclusivity period I will be seeking offers from other companies, which tends to draw better offers. If they want your business, they will pay more to have it taken off the table."

14. If the prospect chooses not to return a letter of intent or makes an offer that's unacceptable, then your IB will move to your next choice. If the first prospect comes back with a solid offer, then it will be given a chance to do due diligence and produce a quality of earnings, or Q of E, report. The prospect sends in the accountants to go over your books and make sure your financials are clean and accurate. They will check to see that inventory has been counted correctly, that personal expenses billed to the business are appropriate, and so on. Any questionable financial findings—excessive personal expenses, overstated earnings, suggestions of withheld information—are what's known in investment banking circles as "hair." Too much hair can kill a deal.

15. While the Q of E report is being generated, the buyer's attorneys will write the purchase agreement, which will usually be from thirty to fifty pages long. As the seller, you will respond to the agreement, confirming that it aligns with the letter of intent. Review all terms, including such things as deferred payments and noncompete clauses. The purchase agreement will include representations and warranties (or "reps and warranties"), which stipulate that what you are telling the buyer about your business is true. For instance, you're stating that to the best of your knowledge, your contracts are up to date and will not be invalidated by the transaction, there is no pending litigation against your company, etc. Anything you know that could potentially be harmful, you must disclose. If you fail to do so, your buyer could take you to court after the sale closes and ask for damages.

16. If all your numbers check out, then the buyer lines up financing and both parties endorse the purchase agreement. You can close on that day, or if the agreement calls for it, do a future close. With the documents signed, your sale is complete!

A typical deal process lasts six to twelve months from initial engagement of an investment banker to closing.

HOW YOU'LL BENEFIT

Did I mention you'll get the most money with an external transfer? That's the biggest benefit of selling to either a strategic or a financial buyer. But there are others.

If you're not 100 percent ready to step away from your company, one of the most compelling motives is the *private equity recapitalization*, or "recap." Remember, private equity groups (PE groups) buy strictly based on their likely return on investment; they want to increase the value of the business and then resell it for a profit. In a recap, a private equity group typically buys 60 to 80 percent of the equity in a business and the owner retains the other 20 to 40 percent. The owner is asked to stay on for five to seven years—a common holding period for private equity. The PE group will then turn around and sell the business. At that point the business owner gets a second liquidity event, or what we call a "second bite at the apple."

This is a very desirable option for owners who still have a fire in their belly and aren't ready to retire but want to take some chips off the table. A private equity recap can be very lucrative; if the business experiences robust growth in those five to seven years, the owner's remaining 30 percent could fetch him more money at his second liquidity event than his 70 percent did at the initial sale! This is because PE groups are highly skilled at acquiring and growing companies and then selling them at a substantial profit.

The downside is that you're no longer the majority shareholder, so you're not calling the shots. Make sure your ego can handle that before you pursue a recap.

Recaps are much more common with business-to-business companies and in industries like manufacturing where PE groups are typically able to improve operations by building strong management teams. They are less common with service businesses like law firms or medical practices, which very often are owner-operated.

The other main benefit of selling to an outside buyer is reliability. You're dealing with a company that has the resources to finance the transaction and give you cash at closing. When you sell to family or employees, you may find yourself having to carry some kind of seller financing, which means no big payout on closing. An entrepreneur is an entrepreneur, not a bank. You shouldn't be in the financing business.

Finally, an external transfer lets you make a clean break and move on to your next venture, whether that's retirement or a new business. You walk away with (hopefully) millions in the bank, and you're not faced with the prospect of being forced back into the business if your kids or employees run it into the ground. With an external transfer, at worst you might be asked to stay on during a twelve- or twenty-four-month transition period, but that's a small price to pay for a potentially extraordinary payout.

Of course, there are risks involved as well: You may not have built sufficient value to interest a third party. Or your company may be too small to interest an investment banker, in which case a business broker might be a better option. Owners often turn to internal transfers because they have no other near-term options.

Rumors of a sale can also hurt business prospects and undermine employee morale. If you are deeply entrenched with your customers, they might balk at the idea of continuing to do business with the new owners. What if some employees passed up opportunities to work elsewhere because they have a relationship with you or like the internal culture? When the possibility of a sale is introduced, those factors become unstable, causing some employees to look for other jobs.

Waiting to sell also puts you at the mercy of the M&A market. The market normally runs in cycles of roughly five years. During booms, companies fetch the highest multiples. During recessions, your multiples, revenues, and EBITDA will all be compressed. If you sell during such times, you'll sell at a significant discount compared to potential prices during the boom periods.

WHAT TO DO

1. Start working on your value drivers. If you don't have an exit team, build one: CPA, financial advisor, and M&A attorney. You won't hire an investment banker until you're ready to

look for a buyer, but the rest of these professionals will help you increase your company's value and make it more sellable.

2. Monitor the M&A market. The cycles tend to follow the economy and the stock market. For example, valuations and multiples were down substantially in 2008 and 2009, when the Great Recession was at its worst. If you see signs that the market is weakening, it might make sense to sell a little sooner than you had planned in order to get a higher multiple.

3. Also monitor changes in your niche. Industries can fall out of favor fast. I had a prospective client who was in the debt collection business. Unfortunately, his niche was collecting on bad checks, and check use has dropped dramatically due to electronic bill pay. By the time he came to me, he had waited too long. His business was pummeled. His company was doing pennies on the dollar compared to revenue just ten years earlier. If you're in a fast-changing industry and you're not ready to sell ahead of the change curve, your business could take a hit. The worst thing you can do is go blithely on without ever questioning the strategic direction of your company.

If you're able to look a few years down the road and adapt to what is coming—or sell now—you can exit smiling while other owners are wondering what happened.

 **EXIT 911** Start asking about investment bankers. Odds are, your CPA, financial advisor, or M&A attorney will be able to refer you to some investment banking firms that are reputable and whose work they respect. Plan on taking some investment bankers out to lunch and finding someone with the experience and approach you're looking for. Better yet, let them pick up the lunch tab.

Did You Know...?

Business brokers commonly charge their clients a commission percentage twice that of an investment banker to sell the business. That's because brokers are usually willing to sell companies too small for an investment banker to touch—i.e., companies with less than $3 million in revenues.

IF YOU CAN'T (OR WON'T) SELL, CONSIDER AN INTERNAL TRANSFER

Your story is the greatest legacy that you will leave to your friends.

It's the longest-lasting legacy you will leave to your heirs.

—STEVE SAINT, ENTREPRENEUR, AUTHOR, AND PILOT

THE FACTS

There are other ways that a business can change hands. Transactions in which a business is gifted or sold to family members or employees are known as *internal transfers*, and there are several types:

» *Transferring to family members.* The most common method of family transfer is to gift small shares of ownership to your heirs annually within the IRS's tax-exempt gift limit. No money changes hands.

» *Selling to family members,* usually at a substantial discount versus selling to a third party.

» *Selling to a group of your own managers,* also usually at a substantial discount.

» *Using employee stock-ownership plans (ESOPs),* which (if done right) can offer the greatest benefit of any of these options. An ESOP allows employees to gradually acquire shares in the business through tax-deductible contributions to a company-established trust.

What these exit paths have in common is that they involve transferring ownership of your company to a party that you already know, rather than seeking and vetting an outside buyer. But why would an owner choose to do this? Sometimes, the owner has an emotional attachment to the company and has always intended to pass it on to his or her children. Business owners who are interested in passing on not just their company but their values tend to place just as much emphasis on building a legacy as they do on walking away with the most money possible.

Other owners care deeply about their employees and want to take care of them. After all, if you started a business twenty years ago and the core of employees who started it with you are still there, they're family, too. You've been through the wars together. The emotional attachment is deep. Selling a company under such circumstances can breed fear and resentment in longtime employees. Some may wonder if they'll be downsized or if the company will be the same after you leave. That's one of the main reasons some owners choose to sell to employees through a direct purchase or an ESOP.

Then there are the owners who have no choice. Remember, the vast majority of entrepreneurs would choose a sale to a third party for the highest price. But sometimes that choice isn't available. Perhaps the owner is too involved in every transaction, making the business seem less attractive to outside buyers. Maybe the M&A market is soft. Whatever the reason, there isn't a third-party buyer to be had. If you find yourself in that situation, you have two options: Wait for things to change, or do an internal transfer and get the best deal you can.

The majority of internal transfers happen because the company is not sellable. The most common reasons are as follows:

» The company is too dependent on the owner.

» Its industry growth is weak.

» Its financials are neither clean nor updated.

» It doesn't have a strong management team.

» It doesn't have business processes in place that are repeatable and teachable.

» It's too small.

Make no mistake: For most business owners, an external transfer will be the preferable exit path. It yields more money and—when handled correctly—minimizes or eliminates headaches such as seller financing. In reality, however, a third-party sale is not always possible. When an owner is nearing retirement age with a company that is not sellable on the open market, he or she has only three options: stick with the business for years and try to build its sellable value, liquidate and walk away with nothing, or do an internal transfer.

If you are considering an internal transfer, whether because you're out of options or because you want to take care of family or employees, you will always walk away with less money than in a third-party sale. If you can live with that, keep reading.

THE SECRET

The trick is in choosing the internal transfer path that best meets your goals. Your ideal path will differ depending on why you're considering an internal transfer over an external sale. First, let's look at the business owner who cares deeply about passing his business down to his heirs and having them carry on his legacy.

You have two basic options here: gifting the business to your heirs or selling it to them. But within those two alternatives are even more choices.

Gifting

Gifting your business to your heirs is exactly what it sounds like: giving away your interest in your company to your children using the IRS's rules for tax-free asset transfer. This is a common method of passing on a business, but it requires some forward-thinking estate planning. As you might expect, if you simply gave your entire $10 million business to your kids in one fell swoop, they would pay heavy estate taxes if the value of the gift was above the IRS's estate tax threshold, which in 2014 is $5.34 million.

One way to avoid those taxes is to gift each child shares worth a maximum of $14,000, which is the IRS's annual maximum tax-free gift limit. The trouble is, if you have a $10 million company, giving it to your kids $14,000 at a time is going to take forever.

Fortunately, there are strategies that allow you to gift shares worth more than $14,000 without getting pummeled by the IRS. One of the most common is to establish a *family limited partnership*—a legal entity with both general and limited partnership interests. You transfer the business to this partnership and keep the general partnership interest yourself. This allows you to run the business on a day-to-day basis and gift the limited partnership interest to family members over time. Because you are giving minority shares to your heirs, you may be able to reduce their value for tax purposes by applying discounts for lack of control (your heirs don't own a controlling interest in the company) and lack of marketability (they can't sell their shares). This completely legal trick can help you transfer interest in your company while reducing your tax burden.

There are two major downsides to gifting your business to your heirs. The first is obvious: You get no money for your company. If you're counting on selling your business to fund the next stage of your life, gifting is a dead-end street. You may have the satisfaction of watching your kids take over your company, but you will not earn retirement income from it. If you have not invested a retirement nest egg using a tax-deferred account such as a 401(k), this could be a serious problem.

Second, as I mentioned earlier, your heirs may not care about running your company or may lack the skills and knowledge necessary to do so. There's a reason only about 1 percent of family-owned businesses successfully pass on to the third generation: The second generation doesn't have the same enthusiasm you do. It's not really *their* company. It's just cash flow. So before you consider gifting (or selling to your heirs, which I'll discuss in a moment), it's essential that you find out whether they're even interested in running your company.

If the kids *are* interested, make sure they know the company backward and forward years before they need to assume control. Additionally, recommend that your heirs join one of the CEO peer groups I mentioned earlier, such as Young Presidents' Organization, Entrepreneurs' Organization, or Vistage. These organizations will give them access to an advisory board of fellow business owners who have an interest in improving the quality of each other's businesses. This support network can be a huge benefit to your children, especially once you're no longer interested in running the show or in spending a lot of time and energy mentoring them.

Selling to Family

Selling your business to family members may sound great, but it's fraught with pitfalls. The first is that, based on my experience, it's extremely unlikely your heirs will have the cash to buy your company or the ability to get financing. This means you'll have to offer seller financing, and there are no upsides to seller financing. You'll get little cash up front. You'll probably offer the company to your kids at a substantially discounted price, with little or nothing down. And you'll charge them a discounted interest rate. So even if things work out, you'll end up with far less money than in a third-party sale.

The second trap is that your kids will be planning to use company cash flow to make their payments to you. But if they aren't entrepreneurial, or if the employees don't respect them and rebel, the business will falter and you won't get your money. You may have to take control again a few years down the line in hopes of getting something back. That's why I recommend that my clients avoid seller financing at all costs.

The third trap in selling to your kids is that it can ruin relationships. "Even if you're selling to your son or daughter, you have to settle on a price," says Dan Weinmann of EdgePoint Capital Advisors. "I've seen families fight over money as if they don't know each other. It can wreck your relationship."

Despite these pitfalls, a sharp M&A attorney or financial advisor may be able to suggest some ways to make selling to your heirs more palatable. For example, let's say a son is buying out his father—you could turn the sale into a ten-year buyout in the form of a stock purchase. You take all the salary that would have gone to the son for running the company and use it to buy stock from Dad instead. As a stock transfer, the deal would be taxed at the lower capital gains rate instead of at the higher personal income tax rate, giving Dad a nice bump in net income. Another trick is to gift enough shares to your children over time to give them 20 percent ownership of the company. Then, they may be able to take out a Small Business Administration loan using that 20 percent equity as collateral. That would give them the cash they need in order to buy out your remaining shares and let you walk away with something.

These measures are best taken over the long haul so you don't eat away at your estate tax exemption. Every gift worth more than $14,000 per year reduces your $5.34 million exemption by the amount over $14,000. So when it comes to getting your kids to that critical 20 percent mark, slow and steady is the ticket. If you go this route, set up a long-term plan with your financial advisor and tax expert.

Selling to Employees

Your other option for an internal transfer is selling your business to a group of employees. There are two basic options here as well, one of which can have some tremendous benefits—if you do it right.

Management Buyout

A lot of owners are reluctant to sell their businesses to a group of managers because they assume those managers don't have the money to buy the company. In fact, if I ask an owner whether his managers can run the business, and he says yes, my follow-up question is always, "Would they be interested in buying it?" The first answer is almost always "They don't have the money."

Guess what? That doesn't matter. If you have a competent, confident management team, you have options. A private equity group could come in and buy the business and give 5 or 10 percent equity to the managers to carry on running the company. Management gets to ride along as the private equity group builds the company's value and then benefits from the later liquidity event. I've also seen deals where management had no equity but was willing to guarantee debt and bought the company with financing. Bottom line: A great management team won't have a problem getting the money.

Before you consider a management buyout, however, ask yourself honestly whether your key managers can run the business and make it grow. If they can't, don't sell to them. As with a sale to family, you run the risk of being forced to reassume control of a dying business. Ask yourself this: How many vacations have you taken since you started your own business? If the answer is *not many*, then you probably don't have a situation where your managers can run the show on their own. On the other hand, if you've taken plenty of vacations and your managers excel in your absence, then it's possible your presence is actually holding them back. In that case, selling to management could be the best option of all.

ESOPs

The employee stock ownership plan is a management buyout with some substantial tax advantages. There are a lot of misconceptions about the ESOP, and it can be costly and complex to set up. Done right, however, it can be the most beneficial of all the internal transfer options.

An ESOP is like a 401(k) that buys only company stock. It's an independent trust that buys the owner's stock at a price set by an appraiser who has determined the company's fair market value.

Either the ESOP can borrow money to buy the owner's shares of stock, or the corporation can make annual, tax-deductible contributions to the ESOP to buy the owner's stock. The trust holds the stock for the employees at no cost while they are with the company. When they leave or retire, employees can sell the stock back to the company.

The ESOP isn't perfect: You will probably have to accept a lower price for your company than if it were appraised according to its open market value. However, it's all in the timing; in 2009, ESOPs were returning higher values than the open market. One thing is certain: If you have a bank finance the ESOP stock purchase, you won't be able to finance the purchase of all the shares. Typically, a bank will finance the purchase of only one-third to two-third of the owner's shares. The seller can either retain ownership of the rest of the stock or do a seller-financed sale.

But an ESOP is a terrific option for an owner who can't find a buyer, because it gives employees an incentive to help grow the company. Every year, employees will get up to 25 percent of their compensation in company stock. If the company has thrived and the stock has gone up in value, printing press operators can become millionaires. The ESOP is, in part, a government incentive to redistribute wealth to the people who add value to a business.

But the best thing about the ESOP is its tax advantages. No matter how small your company is, the sale is treated as a stock sale, so it's taxed at the lower capital gains rate. Better yet, if the business uses bank financing to purchase the owner's shares, the principal and interest on that loan are tax deductible. Best of all, because an ESOP operates according to the federal Employee Retirement Income Security Act (ERISA), the share of the company owned by the ESOP does not pay income taxes. If an S corporation ESOP owns two-thirds of your $3 million bottom-line business, $2 million of those earnings are not taxed. The business pays taxes on only the remaining $1 million. As the owner, that makes holding on to some of your shares a pretty good deal.

Some advisors will insist that small companies cannot do ESOPs, but the only barrier to establishing one is the cost, though it's not as high as some people think. Creating an ESOP costs about the same as creating and administering a company 401(k): around $10,000 for a small business, and up to about $40,000 for a company with several hundred employees. Also, the business is required by law to pay for an updated annual valuation so it can report to shareholders what their stock is worth.

If you want to sell your company to your employees for the best possible return, an ESOP is a terrific option.

HOW YOU'LL BENEFIT

Despite all these internal transfer options, doing an internal transfer always boils down to one essential fact: You're not going to get as much money as if you sold to an outside buyer. But there are some bright spots. First of all, an internal transfer can help you continue your legacy and perpetuate your core values, if those things matter to you as much as (or more than) your retirement nest egg does. This type of transfer also lets you choose your own buyer rather than putting you at the mercy of the open market.

But the greatest benefit of the internal transfer is that it gives you an exit pathway when selling to a third party just isn't possible. While you may have dreamed of selling your company for $10 million, bad luck and bad planning may have made it unsellable. In that case, a $2 million payday via an ESOP starts to look pretty good.

WHAT TO DO

Start thinking now about whether an internal transfer is right for you. As I've said, most business owners will choose to go after the biggest possible payout, and there's nothing wrong with that. But if you really want to take care of a group of great employees, or you have a son or daughter who's excited about learning the family business, an internal transfer may accomplish your goals.

If you decide that you would like to *gift* your business to your heirs, begin long-term tax and gift planning as soon as possible. If you want to avoid the federal limit on tax-exempt gifts and pass along your company without burdening your kids with a huge tax bill, you'll need to plan years, even decades, in advance.

If you think you want to *sell* your company to your heirs, assume that seller financing will be necessary. That means you'll need to start training one or more of your children to successfully operate the company after you're retired. Develop a plan to get your kids involved, starting at the ground floor and working their way up, learning every aspect of what makes your company tick. Your goal is to leave your business to people who will grow it . . . and spare you years of worry.

If you think a management buyout or an ESOP is the way to go, then start planning ways to make your key managers more effective and more independent. Take vacations. Put in place systems and processes that anyone can operate. You want your top managers to be both capable of taking your company to the next level after the sale and confident enough in their own skills to want to buy it.

Sit down with your financial advisor and discuss your goals for the future. He or she will help you choose an exit option that gives you the best chance of having the financial resources to lead the post-work life you want.

 If you're less than a year out from your desired exit date, it's too late to start a gifting program to your kids. And if they're not already capable of running your company today, selling to them would be foolish. Consider a management buyout or an ESOP, or talk to your financial advisor about charitable exit options such as a charitable remainder trust.

Did You Know . . . ?

According to the National Center for Employee Ownership, about eleven thousand US companies now have employee stock ownership plans in which about 13 million employees own shares.[12]

NEVER SELL YOUR BUSINESS YOURSELF

Sometimes it takes an expert to point out the obvious.

—*SCOTT ALLEN, ONLINE MARKETING STRATEGIST*

THE FACTS

A gentleman (I'll call him "Matt") had built his small Midwestern publishing company into a very successful venture. By 2011 he was publishing six magazines, three community newspapers, and a series of popular e-books focused on local issues, from history to travel. He was doing about $2 million a year in gross revenues, with EBITDA of about $250,000. But at age forty-five, he was growing tired of the business and was ready to move on. He had a solid team of managers behind him, no debt, and strong revenue growth, so he figured it would be a picnic to sell his company himself. He could pocket the commission he'd otherwise pay a broker. Genius!

Matt started off right by hiring a CPA to audit his books and make sure everything was clean. But then he veered off course. Without professional counsel to help him determine a realistic valuation for his business, he went by what he saw on Wall Street: publicly traded companies in similar industries fetching multiples of ten, twenty, and even thirty. He went into the open market asking $6 million for his company, a price that no one in his or her right mind would pay. It's possible that he could've sold for $1 million, but the company was his baby, and Matt had no objectivity.

Well, you can imagine what happened. Word got around that Matt had stuck a ridiculous price tag on his business. He got zero offers. And while he wasted months going to meetings and trying to drum up interest, the market changed. He had taken his eye off the ball. While he was out playing investment banker, there was nobody at the wheel of his company. He lost some key advertisers. The local economy slumped with the closing of a big auto plant. Revenues dropped. In 2012, a year after Matt had made his first foray into the world of do-it-yourself business sales, he was forced to transfer his company to a group of employees for just $500,000, much of it seller financed.

If Matt had gotten some professional guidance, he would have priced his company realistically and probably sold quickly, before his market slumped. Unfortunately, a cottage industry has sprung up around DIY small business sales. If you Google "do it yourself business sales," you'll find a lot of websites pitching their systems for selling your company yourself and saving the cash you'd otherwise pay to those "greedy" investment bankers, accountants, and attorneys.

The trouble is, those investment bankers, accountants, and attorneys know the complexities of selling a business. You don't. Selling even a moderate-sized company involves multiple interlocking levels of tax law, securities law, contract law, financial and estate planning, accounting, and process management. Pitfalls are everywhere, opportunities are easy to miss, and potential liability lurks around every corner. Experienced professionals will help you not only avoid traps but spot opportunities to increase your payout that you might otherwise miss.

To bottom line is this: You are more likely to close a sale, avoid making irreversible financial mistakes, and net more money by selling your business with a team of professionals, even after you factor in their fees.

Even so, this approach remains a hard sell to many small business owners. The smaller a company is, the more likely the owner is to try a DIY sale. Cash flow is tight, and small business owners are already used to doing everything themselves anyway. So they'll negotiate with a buyer and then bring in an M&A attorney at the end to review the contracts. But that means ignoring many critical steps. For example, do you know how to protect your company's confidential information during the sale process? If you don't know the strategies used to protect your trade secrets, your list of key customers, and other vital data, your buyer will exploit that knowledge of your weaknesses to beat you up on price. Going in alone basically cedes control of the transaction to your potential buyer.

These are the most compelling reasons that selling your company yourself is a bad idea:

» *You're too close.* There's a reason that pro athletes and actors have agents: They get more money and better terms when somebody without an emotional connection to the deal does the negotiating. If you have one foot out the door because you can't wait to get to a beach in Maui and start your retirement, who knows what kind of terrible terms you might accept in a purchase agreement? You need professionals negotiating on your behalf so that if a buyer insists on deferred payments (for example), you can negotiate a higher sale price or simply walk away from the deal.

» *You don't know how to arrive at a fair valuation.* You're an expert at running your company, not at pricing it. Unrealistic owner expectations on price are one of the biggest reasons that sales fall through.

» *You don't know how to read the documents.* Do you know what a letter of intent looks like or how to read it? Can you spot small but significant changes in a purchase agreement? Unless you're an experienced M&A attorney, the answer is probably no.

» *DIY selling will devour your time.* You should know by now that it takes twice as long to do something that's outside your area of expertise. So why would you spend endless hours trying to act like an investment banker or a business broker? Who's running your business while you're spending all your time trying to sell it? And what happens to your sale price when your revenues drop while you're running around playing investment banker?

» *You don't know how to recognize a qualified buyer.* Experienced business sales professionals know the difference between a prospective buyer—someone who's got the cash to close and the synergies that make buying your company a sound strategic move—and the "tire kickers" who are likely to ask for seller financing or deferred payments. You, on the other hand, might not.

» *You don't know all the tax implications of your deal.* Taxes can take a huge bite out of your proceeds. And if you pay the wrong amount in post-closing tax, you could get hit with interest and penalties down the line.

Here's another huge potential problem that even most business brokers don't even know about: Selling your stock improperly can get you into hot water with the Financial Industry Regulatory Authority (FINRA), the self-regulatory organization that oversees financial transactions. As you probably know, you need a license to sell securities—shares of stock in a company. Well, there's an ongoing debate about whether selling the *assets* of a private company qualifies as selling securities. That debate could be resolved in the near future. But there's no debate about whether selling the *stock* of a private company qualifies as a securities sale; it does. If you transfer your company via a stock sale but you don't use someone who has the proper Series 7 or Series 79 licensing under FINRA, you could have your transaction rescinded.

Imagine somebody from FINRA calling you a year after your sale closes and saying, "Your sale was invalid. Give back the $8 million." That's a nightmare come to life. Sell your business using licensed, experienced people.

THE SECRET

Assemble a team of professionals who can guide you through the complex process of selling your company—and help you get the price you want and deserve. Don't even consider selling your business yourself. And don't delay—build your team before you need it. I've said it before, but it bears repeating: You can't begin planning for your exit too early.

This is who you'll need on your team and what they will cost you:

First Tier (Your Must-Have People)

» *Investment banker*—Your IB will be the captain of your sale process, but you won't engage one until you are ready to start looking for a buyer. Investment bankers are usually paid based on variations of a formula called the "Lehman Formula," after former investment bank powerhouse Lehman Brothers. Under this formula, your IB will make 5 percent of the first $1 million of your closing price, 4 percent of the next $1 million, 3 percent of the next $1 million, 2 percent of the next $1 million and 1 percent of each $1 million thereafter. (Due to inflation, multiples of the original Lehman Formula are becoming more common. For example: 5 percent of the first $10 million, 4 percent of the next $10 million, and so forth.)

So if your IB sells your company for $6 million and uses the original Lehman Formula, he'll make $50,000 + $40,000 + $30,000 + $20,000 + $10,000 + $10,000 = $160,000. This is known as a *success fee*. Some IBs might charge a flat commission instead, but usually this is still roughly based on what they would get using the Lehman Formula. Some will also ask for incentive fees, which are structured to significantly increase the IB's payday if he or she sells your company at a higher price. "I might take 2 percent up to $10 million," says investment banker Dan Weinmann, "but then take 5 percent over $10 million." Some owners balk at incentive clauses, but trust me, you want your investment banker to be incentivized to get you more money for your company.

» *CPA*—Years before you seek to sell, your certified public accountant will be hard at work maintaining clean financials and making sure your taxes are up to date. Your CPA will also assist your prospective buyer in doing the due diligence and the quality of earnings report. CPAs charge hourly, typically in the $200–$500 range.

» *M&A attorney*—A mergers and acquisitions attorney will help negotiate the terms of your transaction, draft the purchase agreement and other necessary legal documents, help you avoid liability, and assist with regulatory approvals. Depending on whether you work with an associate or a partner, your cost could range from $200 per hour to $500 per hour.

» *Financial advisor*—This is your personal wealth manager, who should ideally carry the CERTIFIED FINANCIAL PLANNER™ (CFP®) designation. Your advisor will help you determine the selling price you need to achieve based on your post-work lifestyle goals. He or she will also set up your estate plan and manage your investment portfolio using the proceeds of your sale. CFP® professionals are typically paid an annual fee of roughly 0.5 percent to 1.5 percent of the assets under management. The range is typically determined by the complexity of your situation and the scope of the services being provided. So if your financial advisor is managing a portfolio with a total value of $4 million, then you will pay him or her between $20,000 and $60,000 per year. Those fees are almost always deducted from your investment portfolio. Avoid financial advisors who are paid on commission. You're looking for a teammate—somebody with a vested interest in your success—not somebody who is operating with a hidden agenda or who is motivated to sell you a product.

Second Tier (Your Might-Need People)

» *Forensic accountant*—If your CPA is not experienced in forensic accounting, it's smart to bring in a firm before your sale to conduct pre-sale due diligence—that is, to review earnings quality, debt, normalized working capital, and other aspects of your financials. A forensic team can also prepare working capital and balance worksheets for your closing. These accountants are paid by the hour, typically from $350 to $500.

» *Tax expert*—Depending on your situation, you might also require the services of either a tax attorney with an LLM

(Master of Laws) in taxation or an accountant specializing in taxation. If your transaction has complicated tax implications, it can be smart to bring in an expert to advise you on structuring your deal in a way that reduces or defers your tax obligation. You'll pay hourly here as well, usually in the $200–$500 range.

HOW YOU'LL BENEFIT

Just invert the reasons you shouldn't sell your business yourself and you'll find lots of reasons that selling with a professional team is a great idea: Less of your personal time is invested, objectivity is more likely to be achieved, you're protected from legal and tax pitfalls, and so on. But two benefits stand head and shoulders above the rest. First, working with an experienced team can protect you from making a financial mistake that can wreck your retirement plans and haunt you for the rest of your life. The sale of company stock by someone without the proper licensing, which I mentioned earlier, is a perfect example. Such a mistake could not only void your sale but financially ruin you and subject you to potential civil and even criminal penalties.

But the best reason to assemble and rely on a team of pros is also the simplest: A group of experienced advisors can and probably will increase the value of your liquidity event. You increase your odds of walking away with a lot more money.

Here's an example: Via a letter of intent, a potential buyer makes an offer for your company that's a certain multiple of EBITDA. But after doing his financial due diligence, the buyer revises your EBITDA downward, reducing the sale price. The reason this sometimes happens is that many privately owned companies do not file tax returns prepared according to generally accepted accounting principles, or GAAP. But a buyer will audit the seller's books based on GAAP, which are strict about such things as inventory costs, payables, and bad debt write-offs. In the end, the seller may have one earnings number while the buyer's auditing team comes back with a lower figure. The result: a lower bid, which looks to the seller like an EBITDA bait and switch. This often leads sellers to withdraw from the deal.

If you're working with an exit team in advance of a sale, these professionals will advise you to perform an internal audit using GAAP and to avoid accounting tricks like bait and switch. In doing so, not only can you correct problems that could cause you to overstate earnings and kill a deal, but you might also discover areas where you can improve cash flow, better manage debt, or reduce expenses, which will increase the value of your company.

Even if the sale of your business turns out to be an exceptionally simple transaction, having your team in place can help you get the most from it. In January 2013, Brad Rosenberg and his partner sold their company—a San Francisco Bay Area sports-marketing and event-planning business focused on the Hispanic demographic—to a much larger competitor with whom they had a friendly working relationship. Following an unsolicited offer, the $1.575 million deal was a no-brainer, Brad says. "A long time ago we had this idea that we would build this asset and then someone would buy it from us and we'd go and do something else," he explains. "But no one was going to pay us a three times multiple for what we'd built. That might have happened before the economy crashed, but not after."[13]

Brad and his partner did their deal without any financial assistance (his partner is an attorney, so they had some legal protection), and they did okay. "We retained majority profit share in the company, diminishing annually until we are out of profit sharing in 2018," Brad discloses. "We also have minority equity in a new entity we created with the new company, and we continue as employees with guaranteed contracts for one year." But he admits that they left money on the table because they knew they would continue to work with the buyer and wanted things to remain amicable. "We could have been much harder negotiators," he says. By selling to an existing business ally, Brad and his partner did pretty well. But they'll never know how much more they could have gotten from the deal if they had brought in a third party and removed the personal aspect from the negotiations.

WHAT TO DO

1. Put your team together and get them going on two projects critical to your exit strategy: an open market valuation of your company and an audit of your financial records based on GAAP. Once that's done, work with your CPA to correct any flaws in your financial reporting, especially if up to now you've been keeping your books on a cash basis.

2. Plan annual meetings at the same time each year, during which you'll discuss your exit planning, strategies to increase the value and sellability of your company, and other relevant issues. Right after those meetings, have your team do updated valuations and financial audits. This will ensure that you have the most up-to-date information possible on earnings and the value of your business. If someone pops up with an unsolicited offer, you'll be prepared.

If you've already received an unsolicited offer or you're getting hints that someone is interested in buying your company, do a thorough presale financial audit now. That will make your business lower-risk and raise its value while reducing the chance of unpleasant surprises.

Did You Know . . . ?

If your business is structured as an LLC or a corporation, you're not done once the closing papers are signed. You'll have a list of things to do, including the following:

» Notify the IRS within thirty days, using Form 966, and close out your employer tax ID number.

» File articles of dissolution with the state where your business was formed.

» Meet with your board and pass a formal resolution to dissolve the company.

Plus, you'll need to attend to important tasks such as paying final bills, canceling insurance policies, notifying customers, and closing business bank accounts.

THERE'S MORE TO A GOOD DEAL THAN THE SALE PRICE

The price of anything is the amount of life you exchange for it.
—HENRY DAVID THOREAU

THE FACTS

Many factors beyond revenues and EBITDA determine the sale price of a business. In the same way, other factors beyond the sale price determine whether a deal is desirable. Understandably, most entrepreneurs looking to sell their business are focused on the number. After all, it's the culmination of all their hard work, and it represents their door to a different life after leaving the company they've built. It's natural that the owner of a business would be primarily concerned with getting the biggest offer possible. However, sale price isn't the only consideration in determining whether a deal is good or bad.

That's why it is so important, as I've already explained, to work with a team of qualified professionals when selling your business. Only experienced pros know the ins and outs of the many ancillary factors that can make or break a transaction. Without their advice, you might find yourself committed to a deal that, while it looks good on the surface, saddles you with a ruinous tax burden, unworkable closing terms, delayed payments, or some other problem.

Having a strong exit team in place is your defense against getting blindsided by nonmonetary aspects of your transaction that could sour your deal or leave you regretting your decision when it's too late to change anything. Selling even a relatively small company is extremely complex, and numerous complications can arise that even many financial professionals miss. For example, not too long ago, I was approached by the owner of a manufacturing business who had already begun negotiations with a prospective buyer. The buyer was offering exactly the amount the owner was looking for: $5 million in cash, with an immediate closing. It looked like a great deal for my new client . . . but it wasn't.

The acquiring company wanted the transaction to be an asset sale; it didn't want to buy the company's stock. But since the seller had created his company as a C corporation, the sale contained a hidden trap: If he had proceeded with the deal as an asset sale, the majority of the proceeds would have been taxed once at the corporate tax rate of 35 percent—and then *again* when the money passed through to my client, at the capital gains tax rate of 20 percent plus the new 3.8 percent Affordable Care Act (ACA) tax. At the end of the day, the seller would have received only about fifty cents on the dollar for his company.

Despite this, his sole focus during negotiations was on price. When I came on board, I set him straight: "You're fighting the wrong battle," I said. "Take the $5 million, but insist that the buyer make it a stock sale." By focusing on the terms of the transaction (rather than the price) and making the deal a stock sale, the seller would pay only the 20 percent capital gains tax plus the 3.8 percent ACA tax. Fortunately, he listened to me—and wound up making seventy-five cents on the dollar after taxes. When all was said and done, that put an extra $1.25 million in his bank account.

This is a perfect illustration of why you can't just focus your attention on the sale price when looking for a buyer or negotiating a sale. Savvy private equity firms and well-advised competitors will come to the table with an arsenal of tricks that can delay your payment and even bind you to the company longer than you'd like. Tax and securities law is filled with potential potholes that can cost you big money or even lead to a lawsuit. Even receiving a quality offer can hurt your ability to extract value, if you get so enamored with that offer that you forget you're always better off having multiple bidders. Having more than one potential buyer chasing after your company is like being the most popular girl at the dance: Eventually, whichever suitor wins is going to have to buy you the nicest dinner and the most expensive champagne.

Some entrepreneurs see nothing but the big number at the bottom of the offer sheet. You cannot afford to be one of them. You must take into consideration ancillary factors in order to determine whether an offer is structured to give you the maximum benefit from your sale.

THE SECRET

Look beyond the price being offered for your business, to the other factors of the offer that can make your exit either a dream or a nightmare—and address them before you make an irrevocable commitment. Falling in love with the dollar figure in your buyer's offer is like falling in love with a house without considering the neighborhood, the schools, the local crime rate, or the property tax rate. You might end up with a terrific Craftsman bungalow ... only to find that it's in the flight path of the nearby international airport and that you can't park your car on the street for fear it will be vandalized.

When considering a purchase offer, you must take into account any conditions the potential buyer might be trying to insert in the agreement. I describe these factors below so you can judge any offer with greater clarity.

Earn-Outs

Earn-outs are conditions written into a purchase agreement that make the payment of some of the owner's money contingent on some future event. For example, if you're selling your company for $4 million, the buyer might insist on tying $1 million of that money to future sales or earnings hitting certain benchmarks. Earn-outs are a way of deferring part of the cost of buying your company until a later date.

Earn-outs are more common when selling a small business—say, one with less than $1 million in EBITDA. Because smaller companies represent more risk for the buyer, some buyers will try to defray that risk by spreading out payments via earn-out clauses. A buyer may also ask for earn-outs when there's concern about the validity of the seller's financials. If the buyer likes the company's other fundamentals but is worried about revenues, the purchase agreement might link future payments to hitting revenue growth goals that were implied in financial documents.

The downside for you, the seller, is that the future is uncertain. You might be prepared to sign off on a $5 million deal with 20 percent of the money in earn-outs because you're thinking, *Of course we'll hit those numbers.* But what if there's an economic downturn? What if the founder of your company's largest customer dies? Not to mention that you're no longer calling the shots and making the decisions that would assist the company in hitting those numbers.

The other red flag about earn-outs is that buyers often structure them so they are hard to hit. If your company has never shown 30 percent year-over-year growth in revenues before, but you agree to defer part of your compensation until the company reaches that 30 percent goal, you may never see another dime and have no recourse but legal action.

My advice: Don't depend on earn-outs to get a buyer on the hook. They can be used as deal sweeteners (adding a bonus to your sale price if the company shows truly robust growth after you leave, for example), but that's all. Simply put: If someone needs to defer a large chunk of the cost of buying your business, he or she is not a player.

Installments

An *installment sale* can be a good thing—if you can afford to wait for your money. It's what it sounds like: You agree to a sale price, but you receive your money on a set schedule spread out over several years. This can have advantages for both the buyer and the seller:

> » It allows *the buyer* to use cash flow from the business to make the payments, reducing the chances of a default.

» It might mean *the seller* pays a lower rate on the smaller payments. Payments are taxed when they're received. So if you're paying income tax on the sale proceeds (instead of capital gains tax), you may pay a lower rate on the smaller payments.

Installments might not be right for you, however, if you need your money all at once in order to fund your post-work lifestyle or start another business, or for some other reason. Also, there's the risk of default: What if your buyer defaults on installment payments? You might find yourself up to your neck in litigation when all you want to do is relax and enjoy your retirement.

As with earn-outs, a buyer's desire to purchase your business in installments can be a red flag that the deal is not right for you. A buyer who wants to extend installment payments out over an unrealistic period (say, twenty years) is not a player, and you should look elsewhere. In all cases, proceed with caution.

Tax Implications: Asset Sale vs. Stock Sale

Taxes can devastate your return from the sale of your company, so part of your exit planning must involve minimizing your tax burden. You can pay the ordinary income tax rate, which currently tops out at 39.6 percent, on your sale. Or you can pay the capital gains tax rate, which currently tops out at 20 percent, on your sale. Which would you rather pay?

Whenever possible, any transaction between you and your

buyer should be structured to give you the maximum tax advantage. That's why it's so important to have a CPA working with you to review the potentially enormous tax implications of any deal. In my earlier example—the client who owned a manufacturing company—you saw the potential impact of selling assets versus selling stock.

First, let me specify what I mean by *assets* and *stock:*

» In an *asset sale*, the seller retains the legal rights to the corporation and to nontransferable property like trademarks and patents, and the buyer takes possession of the assets owned by that corporation. These can include accounts receivable and accounts payable, equipment, trade secrets, licenses, inventory, and customer databases. If a business is structured as a sole proprietorship, a partnership, or a limited liability company (LLC), then the transaction *must* be structured as an asset sale.

» A *stock sale* is available only to S and C corporations. The buyer purchases both the legal corporate entity and all the corporate stock (this does apply to privately held companies, since they often issue shares).

In general, buyers prefer asset sales, while sellers prefer stock sales. Asset sales tend to favor the buyer because it can take depreciation on the acquired assets, reducing the buyer's tax obligation and increasing cash flow. In addition, because the buyer is acquiring assets but not the actual corporation, the buyer doesn't have to worry about also acquiring unknown legal liabilities such as contract disputes or employee litigation.

Asset sales are not as good for sellers because, as I mentioned earlier, the proceeds are mostly taxed as ordinary income rather than as capital gains. And as we saw with the manufacturer, if the company is a C corporation, then the proceeds will be taxed twice.

When it's an option, sellers usually prefer a stock sale, especially if the business being sold is a C corporation. Stock sales are taxed at the much lower capital gains rate, giving you (the seller) more money at the end of the day. Also, because the buyer is acquiring the rights to the corporate entity itself, a stock sale typically reduces or eliminates the seller's future liability in areas such as pensions and product liability claims.

Buyers don't like stock sales as much because they cannot take depreciation on the acquired assets, and because in buying the corporation they open themselves up to a wide range of possible future liability, from employee discrimination lawsuits to environmental violations.

Most purchases under $10 million are structured as asset sales, both to reduce risk on the part of the buyer and because such entities are frequently neither S nor C corporations. But if your company is an S or a C corporation, making a stock sale a possibility, the question comes down to negotiation. In order to get your buyer to agree to make the transaction a stock sale rather than an asset sale, you may have to give on price or another issue (like earn-outs or deferred payments). This is why you should go over your options with your legal and accounting advisory team early in the process, and go into negotiations knowing what you want.

Nondisclosures

Nondisclosure agreements (NDAs) are standard operating procedure in M&A negotiations, and you and your buyer will typically sign one at the beginning of the process. They are used to protect confidential or proprietary information (trade secrets, manufacturing processes, etc.) during negotiations, so they are generally a positive aspect of the sale process.

However, if you are negotiating to sell your business to a supplier, customer, or competitor, then you likely will be asked to reveal most of your trade secrets at some point in the negotiations. Though you are under the protective umbrella of your NDA, giving you legal recourse should your prospective buyer steal your trade secrets when the deal falls through, some buyers are reluctant to lay all their cards on the table like this.

The purpose of the nondisclosure agreement is to protect the seller, not the buyer. If your prospective buyer balks at signing an NDA at the outset of negotiations, then do not proceed with the deal and do not reveal confidential information, including financials.

Noncompetes

Noncompete agreements (NCAs) are also common in business sale negotiations, but they can have more serious implications for the seller than the NDA does. The noncompete simply warrants that the signer will not become a competitor of the company purchasing the business for a set period of time after the sale closes (typically three to five years). The terms of an NCA can range from strict (barring you and your employees from working in the same industry as the company you just sold) to relatively lenient (barring you only from starting a new business in the same industry), but they generally focus on protecting the buyer from any attempt to steal their clients.

Most buyers will insist that your employees have signed NCAs on file. This makes your business appear less risky and will likely increase its value. You'll also be expected to sign one so that you can't steal your old clients or employees away from the new owner.

The noncompete is pretty much mandatory in any transaction, but that doesn't mean you should come to the table unprepared to negotiate on terms. Think about it: Do you really want to make a legal commitment not to work in the industry where you've spent the last several decades of your life? This presents a problem for many business owners. Before you sign an NCA, be sure you can live with the restrictions and the period that the agreement is in force. If you can't, negotiate.

HOW YOU'LL BENEFIT

The benefits of paying close attention to all the nonprice aspects of your transaction come down to one thing: a successful sale that you can be happy with. I don't consider it a good outcome if a buyer sells for his $10 million asking price but then is prohibited from working in the industry that he loves. If you get hit by double taxation because you didn't understand the implications of being a C corporation, someone on your exit advisory team isn't doing his or her job.

Working with your team to monitor and prepare for all these eventualities can help you do the following:

» Walk away with more money in your pocket after your transaction is done

» Minimize your tax obligation

» Extract the maximum value from your hard work

» Avoid future litigation

» Enjoy a smoother, faster selling process

» Avoid unpleasant surprises

» Come to negotiations better prepared to put together a win-win deal that ensures a successful closing

Remember, at the end of the day, a successful sale is one that leaves you feeling satisfied with the *overall results*, which means more than just the number on the check.

WHAT TO DO

I'm going to assume you've taken my advice from earlier secrets and put together your exit strategy team. If you haven't discussed your tax status, your interest in earn-outs, and your tolerance for things like noncompete agreements, have that discussion. Before you ever start soliciting offers for your company, have a basic idea of where you stand on every one of these issues.

Tom Harrison, CPA, managing director of Westlake, Ohio–based accounting firm Corrigan Krause, recommends some additional areas that require the attention of both buyer and seller. Based on nearly three decades of experience in buying and selling businesses within the closely held business community, he has found that a few major factors—apart from price—determine whether a deal works. Addressing these factors will help you arrive at the true value of the deal on the table:

1. *Do your due diligence.* Tom advises thorough due diligence investigations by both the seller's and the buyer's sides:

   Both parties should do the proper investigation. Buyers should rigorously verify things like assets, liabilities, operational issues, and profitability. However, most entities will have entered into a number of agreements and contracts by the time they are ready to sell. Such contracts may put restrictions on a deal that may not initially be evident. That's why the completeness of the due diligence process can't be overemphasized.

Tom suggests that sellers focus on verifying the buyer's ability to finance the purchase, its integrity in other financial dealings, and its ability to manage the company profitably if the deal is done (something that can come into play if a seller agrees to earn-outs or profit sharing). He offers an example:

> We had a situation where we were 98 percent complete with a deal representing the buyer. Announcements were made, employee meetings took place, documents were signed, marketing materials were in process, human resource issues were being addressed, and culture issues were being taken care of . . . and then we had a last-minute surprise. It turned out that one of the seller's major vendors had entered into an agreement more than twenty-five years earlier that gave the vendor first right of refusal to buy the company. That agreement didn't show up in due diligence. The sellers didn't remember it, but their signatures were on it. The vendor ended up buying the company, and our client lost both time and money.

2. *Be honest with yourself.* Tom also counsels prudence for both buyers and sellers in dealing with the emotions surrounding

the transaction. "Buyers should engage in a thorough inter-rogation of the seller to ensure that he is ready to sell," he says. "The seller should also question the buyer to confirm that he is ready to buy. Nobody enjoys wasting time in mean-ingless negotiations."

Tom cites another example in which his firm was representing a seller and had the deal 90 percent of the way to consummation:

> Key employee conversations had taken place, docu-ments were prepared and ready to be signed, and the seller had even identified his next business venture. Then, at the last minute, it all fell apart. The owner was going to receive exactly what he wanted finan-cially, but he admitted that he just wasn't ready to sell. He felt tremendous loyalty to his family, employees, customers, and vendors, and he realized it wasn't time. He was just beginning to have fun, turn profits, and get some of the stressful parts of his business under control. Ultimately, in the attorney's office the day of closing, he decided (after a long conversation with me) not to sell. Fortunately, his business continues to be successful to this day.

3. *Complete a properly executed and communicated transi-tion plan.* This document—Tom's final must-have—must tell management, employees, vendors, and customers with

total clarity what will take place after the sale and what they should expect. Leaving one party out of the loop can turn a good deal into a bad one. Tom explains:

> My client was selling a large percentage of his company to his son. The trouble was, there were other nonfamily owners involved as well, and in the closely held business environment, this is a recipe for disaster. In this case, everything that we identify as important— communication to ownership, management, vendors, customers—was executed to a T and with proper lead time. Potential problems never arose. The business continues to flourish today as one of the most successful organizations in its area.

4. *Prepare to compromise.* When you finally get a solid offer from a quality buyer, go over each possible ancillary factor in detail, and be prepared to respond to proposed terms and agreements with your own specific alternatives. You won't get everything you want; negotiation is about both sides giving a little in order to reach mutually acceptable terms. But by being hyperaware of and preparing for the many nonprice aspects of a transaction, you'll increase your odds of entering into a sale that's successful—financially, legally, professionally, and personally.

If you're getting ready to solicit offers or have already received them but you haven't given a second thought to terms and taxes, don't panic. Many owners don't consider these issues until late in the game. That's why you have a team of professionals. Sit down today with your CPA and your M&A attorney and go over each item discussed in this secret. Where do you stand on each, in general? Are earn-outs acceptable, or do you need all your money now? If you have the option of doing a stock sale, does that make sense? Go over all the eventualities so there are no surprises.

Did You Know . . . ?

» The enforceability of noncompete agreements varies from state to state. For instance, California prohibits them entirely.

» In some cases, you might be able to substitute a "nonsolicitation agreement" for a noncompete. This prohibits you from hiring former employees or approaching your current company's customers but allows you to start or invest in a business in the same industry.

» Earn-outs can also be substitutes for noncompetes. Having an earn-out based on revenue growth, for example, gives you an incentive not to compete against your former company, because your deferred compensation depends on the company's growth and prosperity.

PART III

PRESERVING VALUE

HAVE A FINANCIAL ADVISOR CREATE YOUR PERSONAL FINANCIAL PLAN

For all long-term investors, there is only one objective:

maximum total real return after taxes.

—JOHN TEMPLETON, STOCK INVESTOR,

BUSINESSMAN, AND PHILANTHROPIST

THE FACTS

Some time ago I was interviewing an entrepreneur who would become one of my company's new financial planning clients. During our conversation, this gentleman told me he had already met with a financial planning firm that had put together a portfolio reflecting the value of all of his investments. He handed me the document, and I began looking it over. Securities? Check. Savings? Check. Real estate? Check. But something huge was missing.

"This financial plan is completely inaccurate," I told the prospect, whose eyebrows went up. I explained to him that the other firm had left something out: *his business!* In developing a financial strategy for his future, they had completely ignored an asset worth more than $2 million—more than half his net worth. By overlooking his business, the other firm had made it impossible to develop an accurate or sustainable financial plan for the next twenty years of his life.

This isn't an uncommon predicament. There are a lot of financial advisors who simply manage investments—not the value of somebody's business. Even if they did remember to include the value of a privately held business, many such advisors wouldn't know how to value it and would simply ask you, which would lead to an inaccurate plan. According to findings from Merrill Lynch's *Affluent Insights Survey: Business Owner Spotlight*, only 35 percent of business owners with $10 million to $250 million in revenue are "very confident in their personal wealth management strategy's ability to meet their financial and life goals if they were to stop running their business today."[14]

It may be surprising that such successful individuals have so little confidence in their financial plans, but a Columbia Business School white paper titled "Life After an Exit: How Entrepreneurs Transition to the Next Stage" explains why this might be the case:

> The qualities that make a good entrepreneur are seldom the same ones that make a good investor. Entrepreneurs typically become successful by intense focus and concentration within a narrow domain and active management to control risk. The principles of successful wealth management are quite different, with an emphasis on diversification and relying on the expertise of others.[15]

The truth is, many of the qualities that make you a great entrepreneur can actually sabotage your chances of enjoying a comfortable, secure retirement. Not to mention that many business owners who have been using the cash flow from their companies to cover their personal expenses are not ready for the income restrictions that come from living off the proceeds of their business sale.

Suppose you run a company with $8 million in annual sales and a current market valuation of $3.2 million. What would your annual income look like if you sold the company for the full $3.2 million and then withdrew 4 percent of the money per year (the withdrawal amount that gives your nest egg the best chance of lasting for the rest of your life)? Let's quickly do the numbers:

Total annual sales	$8,000,000
EBITDA of 10%	$800,000
Sale price of four times EBITDA	$3,200,000
Capital gains taxes, investment banker commission, and other fees (about 30%)	$960,000
Your net liquidity event	$2,240,000
Your annual income (withdrawing 4% annually)	$89,600

Could you live on $90,000 a year (plus Social Security, if you're old enough to collect) for twenty-five years? More to the point, would you want to put yourself and your family in a situation where you had no choice other than to go back to work? That's often the hard reality for business owners who base their entire retirement plan on the sale of their business. As we have already seen, many businesses are not worth as much on the open market as their owners believe.

Faced with this reality, an entrepreneur working closely with a financial advisor can take steps to prevent a massive income falloff in retirement. By setting up and making regular contributions to a qualified, tax-deferred retirement account like a Simplified Employee Pension (SEP), which allows you to save more than $50,000 per year, or to a defined benefit plan (a pension plan), which allows savings of well over $100,000 a year, you can supplement any income you might receive from selling your business. That's one way a financial advisor can help you in the long term.

But if you neglect to put together a personal financial strategy that includes retirement savings and wealth management, you're putting your future at the mercy of the M&A market, your customers, and the general unpredictability of the economy. If you're older, that vastly increases the risk that you and your spouse won't have enough money to live on in your retirement. If you're younger, you take a greater risk that your plans to fund your children's college education and use some of your sale proceeds to start another company will fall flat.

That's because entrepreneurs face an array of unique financial planning challenges:

» *Higher risk and volatility.* According to statistics published by *Inc.* in its December 2012/January 2013 issue, 67 percent of small business owners worry they won't be able to put away enough money for retirement.[16] Compare that to just 38 percent of non–business owners who say the same. Entrepreneurs have the potential for a much higher payout than the average rank-and-file employee who draws a steady paycheck, but they also have incomes that are far less predictable.

» *Lack of liquidity.* On average, 80 percent of an entrepreneur's net worth is tied up in his business. Additionally, entrepreneurs tend to reinvest much of their excess cash flow back into the business, as opposed to investing it outside of the business.[17]

» *Lack of diversification.* If 80 percent of your net worth is concentrated in your business, this means that 80 percent of your assets are allocated to a single micro-cap company. No sane investor would invest 80 percent of his or her principal in micro-cap stocks; the risk of a catastrophic loss would be too high.

» *Uncertainty of income.* During recessions, which typically happen every four to five years, revenues and profits decrease considerably. During such tough times, the first thing to be sacrificed is often the business owner's paycheck. This makes it more likely that as the business owner you'll be earning less income, making it difficult to save for retirement.

» *Ignorance of a business's value.* Based on my experience, I'd estimate that more than 75 percent of entrepreneurs do not know the market value of their businesses. Since an entrepreneur's business typically comprises such a significant portion of his or her net worth, that's a problem. Not knowing the company's value today makes it impossible to manage the company to increase its sellable value over the long term.

When you add to the equation the entrepreneur's single-minded focus on running his or her business to the exclusion of all else, it should come as no surprise that many business owners suffer from a woeful lack of personal financial planning. In fact, according to the same *Inc.* survey, nearly one-third of small business owners say they will not be able to retire until after age seventy.

Every entrepreneur should work closely with a financial advisor to develop his or her financial strategy for the exit and beyond. Think about it this way: After the sale of your business, your investment banker will have moved on to another client. Your CPA and your M&A lawyer will no longer be working for you. Your financial advisor is the only person on your exit team who will be thinking about your financial welfare beyond the close of your business sale.

Despite this, according to findings from the Merrill Lynch survey, only 33 percent of business owners have worked with a personal financial advisor or a commercial banker to prepare their personal finances "for possible scenarios in which they will no longer be actively running their business." That's a terrible oversight. If you want a successful exit and transition to post-work life, you need to start by getting your personal financial house in order.

THE SECRET

Any sound exit and wealth management strategy must begin with engaging a financial advisor who has extensive experience working with entrepreneurs and planning for business exits. Creating your personal financial plan is not a do-it-yourself proposition. Sure, you might be able to manage your small portfolio of mutual funds or individual stocks for a few years, or even open a 401(k) or a SEP plan. But when you're running a business, things quickly become too complex for the layperson. Not to mention that you might not even have time to make your bank deposits, much less spend hours rebalancing the assets in your retirement plan.

At the end of the day, a comprehensive personal financial strategy is about much more than establishing and managing a portfolio of investments for the maximum return. It's about strategies that minimize your tax obligation without letting the IRS take you to the woodshed. It's about ensuring that you're taking care of your family with things like college savings and estate planning. Most important, it's about creating a long-term plan that increases the value of your most important asset— your business—so that when you sell, you'll have the cash flow you need to live the life you want.

But how do you choose a financial advisor who's right for you? Or if you're already working with an advisor, how do you know whether he or she is the person to guide you to and beyond your exit?

First, if you're currently working with an advisor, try this simple test: Ask him or her to provide an open market valuation of your business. If your advisor can't do that, it's a dead giveaway that he or she has never taken a client through an exit process. Faced with the complexity of tax planning, estate planning, payout schedules, and all the other factors that come into play, an advisor with no exit experience will not be prepared to develop an effective personal financial plan.

If your current advisor doesn't have the experience you need, you should strongly consider ending that relationship and moving on. It's nothing personal; the person who got you started twenty years ago saving money in a Roth IRA or 401(k) might not be the person to guide you through the most significant financial event of your lifetime. It's time to find someone else.

Where to start? Well, whether you're looking to hire your first financial advisor or replace your current one, you should start with the relationship. Look for an advisor who's interested in you as a person, not just as a collection of numbers. CPAs and investment bankers might come and go, but you might work with your financial advisor for twenty years or more. It can be an intimate, highly personal relationship. You don't want someone who's more interested in the size of your portfolio than in whether you are reaching your lifelong aspirations.

An advisor's interests will be apparent to you at the first meeting. Someone whose initial questions are all about statements, rates of return, amounts saved, and so on is probably a quantitative thinker—i.e., someone focused more on the numbers than on the person. Sure, you want your advisor to have strong quantitative skills, but anyone who is licensed should be proficient in the quantitative side of things. The fact that someone sits down and calculates your investment return on his or her financial calculator should not impress you.

The financial advisor you want is someone who is interested in you as a whole person. This type of advisor will ask about things like your goals, motivations, passions, dreams, and relationships. He'll want to know what you want your life to look like post-exit, what your hopes are for your children (if you have any), and what causes you're enthused about supporting. This type of advisor will get to know you and your family and will probably become a trusted financial partner.

You should also look for someone who offers not just investment management but wealth management. *Investment management* is about tweaking your portfolio of securities (stocks, bonds, and other asset classes) to give you the best possible risk-adjusted return. That's important, but it ignores all the other facets of your financial life: taxes, inheritance, philanthropy, insurance, and the value of your business. *Wealth management* is about clarifying your entire financial picture so you have what you need to accomplish all that's important to you, without having to deal with any unnecessary financial stress.

Under the wealth management umbrella, you'll find investment consulting, advanced planning, and relationship management:

» *Investment consulting*—This is the portfolio and asset management aspect of the advisor's work, and it's what most people think about when they think about financial planning. It involves the management of all elements of the client's investments to maximize the probability of the client achieving his or her goals. It includes the following:

  › Portfolio performance analysis

  › Risk evaluation

  › Asset allocation

  › Assessment of costs and impact

  › Assessment of tax and impact

  › Investment policy statements

» *Advanced planning*—These services involve highly complex financial and legal planning tasks. To handle them, the advisor is usually required to rely on a team of other specialists: tax attorneys, CPAs, insurance experts, and others. Advanced planning includes the following:

> Wealth enhancement: tax mitigation and cash flow planning

> Wealth transfer: transferring wealth effectively, within or outside of the family

> Wealth protection: risk mitigation, legal structures, and using insurance to transfer risk

> Charitable giving: maximizing the philanthropic impact of wealth

» *Relationship management*—Your advisor's most important task is to ensure that you feel informed about, confident in, and empowered by the financial planning process. Relationship management is about the regular meetings, ongoing consultation, plan updates, and other activities that keep you and your plan on a steady course. It includes the following:

> Client relationship management: communicating with clients and working as their teammate, not their adversary

> Professional network relationship management: collaborating with a network of key service providers to assess your situation from all angles

Many entrepreneurs mistakenly believe that they need a certain amount of money saved before they qualify for this suite of wealth management services. That's wrong. You don't need millions of dollars in a brokerage account to need a wealth manager, because wealth management isn't just about optimizing wealth. It's about *creating* it. If you only have $120,000 in your 401(k) but you own a company that's doing $5 million in annual revenues, you have plenty of *potential* wealth to manage. Your financial advisor is the person with the skill set and the experience to help you turn that potential wealth into *actual* wealth. So don't wait.

HOW YOU'LL BENEFIT

Surveys conducted by the Consumer Federation of America (CFA) consistently show that people who have a financial plan save more money, make smarter investment decisions, and are more confident in their financial progress, regardless of their income.

Creating your financial plan inoculates you against the volatility of the financial markets. Because your financial advisor is once removed from your portfolio of investments, he or she can make asset management decisions based on your plan and on sound market and economic research, not on the emotion and blind panic that so frequently cost inexperienced investors big money. No matter how cool and calm you think you are, when it comes to your money, it's still *your money*. It represents freedom and sacrifice and everything you've worked for. You can hardly be expected to be objective about it.

I have seen entrepreneurs pull their investments out of the stock market at the bottom—exactly the opposite of what you should do—because they couldn't handle the emotional roller coaster of the kind investors experienced in 2008 and 2009. For an entrepreneur, this would be similar to selling your business at a significant discount in the middle of a recession—when earnings and revenues are deeply depressed—even though you know in your heart that the downturn is just a phase.

History shows that the markets tend to see their greatest increases in value early in the "bounce" period—that inevitable return to positive momentum on the economic charts. By waiting to get back in, you lose money. Fidelity Investments researched people who had been investing in their 401(k) plans for at least ten straight years, through the dramatic financial downturn of 2008. The research shows average annual increases of about 17 percent, up from $46,000 in 2003 to $200,000 in the first quarter of 2013. John Sweeney, executive vice president of retirement and investing strategies for Fidelity, attributed that growth in part to the stock market rebound.[18]

Having a financial advisor's hands on the wheel protects your assets from rash emotional decisions. Advisors live by the guiding principle in investing: *Buy low, sell high*. Your advisor won't let you make a panicked move that will cost you a fortune. He or she will talk you down from the ledge, remind you about things like the historical performance of the S&P 500, and keep you from making terrible financial decisions out of fear.

Additionally, a financial advisor with exit experience will keep your big financial picture in mind. He or she will not only design a wealth management strategy that helps you reach your financial goals but will also work with you to grow your company's value so when you do sell, you'll have the cash you need to live the life you want.

Then there are the factors of time and expertise. If you are operating a growing company, you almost certainly don't have the time to do anything more than glance at an online statement or check your smartphone for where the Dow closed on a given day. You certainly don't have the time to sit down and develop a comprehensive wealth management plan designed to adapt as your needs and the financial markets change over ten or twenty years. You're also not a financial expert. Financial advisors know the markets and financial instruments, have the licensing and training to manage assets legally and prudently, know the tax implications of each transaction, and follow the changes in banking, securities, and tax law.

You wouldn't do your own root canal or represent yourself in court, right? You would engage a skilled professional. Hiring an experienced CFP® professional operating under the registered investment advisor (RIA) umbrella makes the same kind of sense. You'll pay an annual fee in return for the kind of knowledge and finely tuned planning that can make the difference between a luxurious retirement and just scraping by.

This is not just about your personal portfolio, either. A good advisor will help you keep your emotions in check when you're trying to sell your company. For example, if you're asking $4 million for your business and an offer comes in for $2.5 million, you might get so excited at the big number—literally more money than you've ever seen at one time—that you're ready to accept on the spot. Your advisor will say, "Wait a minute. Our financial plan for your retirement is based on selling for $4 million. Unless you want to have to get a job in ten years, let's take a step back."

The best financial advisors focus on more than just managing your investments. They help you optimize the after-tax value of your business and eventually exit it on your own terms. They can perform calculations that will begin at the end point—your goals for your post-exit life and the amount of money that you will need to achieve those goals—and work backward, looking not only at how much you need to get from the sale of your business but also at how much you should be saving in a qualified retirement account. This kind of planning aids you in a number of ways:

» It establishes a firm dollar goal for your eventual exit, giving you a compass with which to navigate your company's growth strategy. If you get a valuation of $3 million today but need to be able to sell your company in three years for

$6 million, you'll know that you need to make some big changes to increase your company's value. On the other hand, if selling for $3 million fits your plan, you can be more prudent and make smaller changes that will enhance sellability without taking undue risks.

» It creates a diversified portfolio of retirement investments beyond the hoped-for proceeds from your liquidity event. This can provide invaluable peace of mind.

» It minimizes your tax burden not only on the proceeds of your sale but also on your income as a business owner. Did you know that in 2014 you could contribute up to $210,000 to a defined benefit plan (depending on your income and your age) and that amount would come right off your taxable income? Even accounts with lower limits, such as personal 401(k) accounts, can knock more than $50,000 off your taxable income. Yet according to the US Small Business Administration, only about 36 percent of US business owners have an IRA—and only about one-third of those actually contribute to the account.[19] That's a huge wasted opportunity to lower your tax obligation.

If you have not yet engaged a financial advisor, look for one who can help you build not just a portfolio but a life strategy. If you're already working with someone who is simply managing your investments but not advising you on taxation, estate planning, or risk management, consider finding someone else who can help you be fully prepared for your exit and what comes after.

Strategist, wealth manager, counselor, voice of sanity, friend—the right financial advisor will become one of the most important people in your life.

WHAT TO DO

When you're ready to select a financial advisor, here are some important tips to start with:

1. *Choose a CERTIFIED FINANCIAL PLANNER™ (CFP®) professional.* CFP® professionals have taken a series of classes on issues ranging from investments and taxes to estate planning. To earn the right to use the designation, they are also required to pass a comprehensive ten-hour exam covering six different areas of finance. The national pass rate is about 55 percent, and only about 20 percent of financial advisors working in the field hold the CFP® professional designation. These folks are the cream of the crop. According to the CFP Board of Standards, 87 percent of clients who work with a financial advisor who holds the CFP® designation are very satisfied, compared with 72 percent who work with an advisor who lacks that certification.

2. *Choose a CFP® professional who also operates as a registered investment advisor (RIA).* The majority of financial advisors do not operate as RIAs, and it's a big differentiator. While other advisors are held only to a *suitability* standard, anyone working as an RIA is held to a *fiduciary* standard. Advisors working under the suitability standard don't have to do what's best for you . . . as long as they don't do anything that hurts you. They are typically motivated by commissions and may recommend products that are in their best interest— but possibly not yours. Under the suitability standard, they are allowed to do this as long as the product gives *some* benefits. A fiduciary, on the other hand is legally bound to do what is in the best interest of the client at all times. An RIA is your partner and teammate, not someone with a hidden agenda or a conflict of interest. Which would you rather have handling your money?

3. *Choose an advisor who works on a fee basis, not a commission basis.* Commission-based advisors are a dying breed, but there are still plenty of them out there. They work with broker-dealers and get paid by buying and selling investments and products and moving them in and out of your portfolio—something that may not always be in your best interest. Fee-based advisors are paid a percentage of your total assets under management. The more your assets grow,

the more they make. So they are incentivized to help you grow your wealth, not to churn your account.

4. *Find out whether the advisor in question has a team of allies, such as CPAs, investment bankers, and M&A attorneys.* These are the people who will help you execute a successful sale of your company, and if your advisor already has people whom he or she trusts, you can start the planning process with your team already in place. That's a huge advantage.

5. *Ask about the advisor's experience working with entrepreneurs and guiding clients through business exits.* Does he or she understand the unique challenges that business owners deal with? Your advisor should know the process that occurs when a business owner puts a company up for sale, from the creation of the business "book" to the final negotiations, and should understand the impact of things such as having a company set up as an S corporation versus a C corporation. If your prospective advisor can't provide that information, move on to someone else.

6. *Find out what the firm's average clients look like.* Nobody wants to be a financial advisor's smallest or largest client. It's not good to be a little fish in a big ocean of wealthier clients; smaller clients tend to receive less attention and service than larger clients do. (Advisors understand the Pareto principle, which explains that 80 percent of their business comes from

the top 20 percent of their clients.) And you probably don't want to be 500 percent bigger than a firm's other clients, because the firm might not have the resources to meet your needs. Ask about the average client's assets under management at the firm so you can make an educated decision.

7. *Go to www.cfp.net (the CFP Board website), where you can check your prospective advisor's credentials.* You can review the advisor's qualifications as well as any disciplinary action or professional sanction that he or she might have received in the past.

8. *Ask for references.* If you're really interested in working with an advisor, ask to speak to some of his or her clients. Get on the phone and talk to them about what the advisor is like to work with, how well he or she listens, how sound his or her financial judgment has proven to be, and how reliable the advisor is about keeping promises. Getting the feedback of people who have nothing to gain by telling you the truth can teach you a great deal about an advisor's character and ethics. If you ask for references and the advisor refuses to provide them, walk away. He or she is hiding something.

9. *Ask a trusted source.* Referrals are the best way to find your advisor. Ask around. Talk to friends and colleagues who have an advisor they really like and then schedule a meeting. I also strongly suggest choosing an advisor who engages in

the following multistage consultative process with prospective clients.

Stage One: Discovery Meeting

The first consultation is designed to uncover your values and priorities and to assess the feasibility of establishing a working relationship. The advisor uses a systematic, detailed interview process to define your financial needs, your goals, and your current position. The result is a total client profile, which the advisor will use to communicate your complete financial picture to the professionals who will execute the recommendations in your wealth management plan.

Stage Two: Wealth Management Analysis Meeting

At your second meeting, your advisor will walk you through your wealth management analysis. It's a diagnostic of your current financial situation, designed to point out the strengths and weaknesses of your position and to help you and your advisor determine how and where to improve your financial standing. This analysis is also a road map that you can follow toward your long-term financial goals.

Stage Three: Mutual Commitment Meeting

During the first part of this meeting, you have the opportunity to ask questions or voice concerns regarding the wealth management analysis. If you are pleased with the answers and with the advisor's recommendations so far, you and the advisor will make a mutual commitment to work together. You will be asked to execute all documents needed to commence the relationship.

Stage Four: Strategic Wealth Plan Meeting

This fourth meeting is the culmination of the consultative process. Your advisor should provide you with the following important documents:

> *Final advanced plan*—A comprehensive evaluation of your current financial condition and recommendations for reaching your financial goals.

> *Market valuation*—An assessment of your company's value to a buyer on the open market.

> *Value driver analysis*—An action plan for optimizing your company's value drivers and increasing your potential sale price.

A good financial advisor will also hold regular progress meetings at intervals that you're comfortable with (quarterly, annually, etc.), where you can review your investment allocation, ensure that your strategic wealth plan is still on course, and reroute and navigate accordingly when changes are appropriate.

This consultative, holistic approach stands in contrast

to the *transactional* approach, where a financial advisor focuses on a single issue, such as investments, and recommends a specific product that addresses a corresponding need. That may work for some clients, but not for the entrepreneur who is looking to exit his or her business.

10. *Provide the necessary input.* Don't think that your work is done once you've found an advisor who uses a multistage consultative process, however. To enable your advisor to provide you with effective personal and business planning, you should consider some other factors:

> *Living expenses*—It's very common for people to underestimate their living expenses. A good way to get an accurate number is to back into the calculation: Figure out what your net paycheck is today. After paying expenses, how much are you saving every month beyond pre-tax contributions to an SEP or 401(k)? If it's nothing, then you're living off 100 percent of what you bring home.

> Don't be fooled by so-called one-time expenses. A client might insist that the $25,000 he or she spent on a new roof shouldn't be considered in figuring their expenses. But if you own a house, there will always be maintenance costs. You'll also vacation, buy gifts, and have other sporadic expenses that still need to be

considered. Once you subtract any retirement savings, the amount you're living on each month is the amount you'll need to be able to draw from your retirement nest egg each month (adjusted for inflation)—unless you want to cut your standard of living.

You must know this number—your monthly living expenses—before you engage in discussions with a potential buyer. If you've decided on that $4 million sale price in order to live the lifestyle you aspire to, you can avoid wasting time in the negotiations when that $2.5 million offer comes in. On the other hand, if your living expenses show that you only need to sell for $2.5 million, you won't hold out for a higher price and risk killing the deal—and possibly burning a valuable bridge.

› *Family Index Number*—Your FIN is the rate of return you must receive on your post-exit investments year after year so you don't run out of money before you run out of life. To ascertain this number, most advisors will also have you complete a risk profile questionnaire. This determines your tolerance for risky investments, which offer higher rates of return but also a greater possibility of losing your principal.

Based on your desired post-exit lifestyle, your other investments, and the likely sale price of your company, your advisor will determine your FIN. A high number usually indicates poor prior financial planning (or no planning) or a desire for a lifestyle that's too lavish to support. If your FIN is 12, that means you need to earn 12 percent each year on your investments, which is difficult to do unless you are willing to tolerate a great deal of risk.

When a client's financial output is excessive—with spending on costly vacations, cars, expensive home renovations, and the like—and the input is small (because the client hasn't saved enough or the business is unlikely to sell for enough), it's reality check time. I have had numerous "come to Jesus" meetings with business owners who thought they would be able to live like the Rockefellers but really had more of a *Simpsons* budget. In that case, they need to accept more risk, radically reduce their lifestyle expectations, or take immediate steps to grow the value of their company.

Then there are the business owners who have invested in a 401(k) prudently for several years, own their home free and clear, and live within their means.

They might have a high tolerance for risk but a FIN of 3. It would be wise for them to scale back their riskier investments while focusing more on preservation of capital and outpacing inflation. I call this "avoiding strikeouts and going for singles." There's more than one way to make it to the Hall of Fame—you don't have to hit home runs to get there.

> *Earn-outs*—If you're looking at a potential sale with earn-outs (deferred payments based on company earnings after you sell), treat them not as the cake but as the icing on the cake. (Go back to secret #8 if you need a reminder of the pros and cons of earn-outs.) If your maximum earn-out is $1 million per year, don't use that number as a benchmark in your planning. Pick a more conservative figure, one-third to one-half of that number. You never know what will happen to your company after you leave. Set yourself up for a pleasant surprise, not a bitter disappointment.

> *Stresstesting*—Nothing ever happens exactly as planned. Because of this, it's important to "stress test" your financial plan. For example, what happens to your plan in the event of death, disability, or an unexpected early retirement? How does your plan work if your first year of retirement turns out to occur during a bear market

that sees stock market returns drop by 20 percent for the year? A solid strategic wealth plan includes measures to keep your financial situation stable under any and all conditions.

11. *Revisit the plan.* Like exit planning, financial planning is not an event but a process. Working with a qualified financial advisor enables you to get the greatest benefit from that process. Consistently revisiting your plan also maximizes the process. Your financial plan is a snapshot in time. Things will change. Your business may not sell for as much as you planned. You may have a good year or a bad year in the stock market. One of your kids might get laid off and need to be bailed out. Life happens. Revisit your plan annually, make sure you have the proper inputs, and understand what your outputs are. You can always make a course correction.

12. *Start today.* Don't wait. Many people are under the assumption that you don't put together a financial plan until you have $100,000 or $1 million in investments, because otherwise it's not realistic. But entrepreneurs are different from the average investor. Even if you don't have a ton of cash, you may have substantial value in your illiquid business. Fully leveraging that asset requires planning—the sooner, the better.

13. *Be true to yourself.* Finally, build a diversified investment portfolio that corresponds with your risk tolerance and is consistent with your Family Index Number. While you may not experience the same returns on your investment portfolio as you would when reinvesting money in your business, you're diversifying your investments (and your risk). You already have a significant portion of your net worth tied up in one micro-cap company—yours—which is an extremely risky investment. This needs to be balanced with a more reasonable investment portfolio that may generate lower returns but with much less volatility.

Don't forget that one of the main reasons your business may generate superior returns is due to the "sweat equity" that you have invested. You've grown used to working for your money. Now it's time to make your money work for you. The best way to make that happen is to create a broad-based wealth management road map with your advisor long before you even need to think about selling.

You can't make a move toward exiting without a valuation of your business. There are several ways of determining your company's value.

One is the "rule of thumb" method, which values a business at a percentage of its annual sales plus inventory. Percentages vary, however, depending on your industry. For example, a dental practice would be valued at between 60 and 65 percent of annual sales plus inventory; a practice with $2 million in sales would be worth $1.2 million to $1.3 million on the open market. Business Reference Guide, published by Business Brokerage Press, lists every important business category along with the accepted percentages to use in determining a valuation.

Another method is to look at the value and multiples of comparable privately held companies that have sold recently. In any case, this is not a DIY project. Provide your financial advisor with complete financials, as well as all the information you can offer on your industry, market, and competition.

Did You Know . . . ?

According to John Leonetti, CEO of Pinnacle Equity Solutions, 80 to 90 percent of most small business owners' personal wealth is tied up in their illiquid small business.[20] That's dangerous, because many business owners have no idea how to convert that illiquid asset into liquid wealth that they can use to support themselves in retirement.

PLAN FOR THE UNEXPECTED

A thing long expected takes the form of the unexpected when at last it comes. —MARK TWAIN

THE FACTS

Many business owners prepare for the unexpected. They install data backup systems, buy fire insurance, and have disaster preparedness plans. But that only protects you and your biggest financial asset from physical catastrophes. Life can change on a dime, and often these changes can be disruptive, fraught with emotion, and potentially damaging to your business. What if your business partner dies suddenly in an auto accident? What if you and your spouse decide to divorce? What if you wake up one day and conclude that you simply don't want to be involved in the business any longer? What happens to your company, your partners, and your future?

Part of a sound, comprehensive exit strategy includes planning for those "what ifs" before they happen. It's a critical aspect of value protection. While we all hope that we will make it to our exit with our health, relationships, and finances intact, it doesn't always work out that way. Life throws us curveballs, and smart entrepreneurs prepare to hit those curveballs before they come—when everything is going smoothly and everyone is calm and getting along. The last thing you want is the future of your company—and your personal financial future—riding on decisions made in the heat of anger or the fog of grief.

Generally, the potential curveballs that can come at a business take the form of what attorneys call "the Five Ds":

» *Death*—What if you or your business partner dies prematurely? How will the business continue without you? How will your family be compensated?

» *Disability*—In the event that either you or your partner becomes physically unable to perform your duties, what happens to the business? What happens to the disabled person's equity ownership in the business?

» *Divorce*—In most states, a business is community property, so it's split between divorcing spouses. What happens when your partner's ex (or yours) becomes part owner of your company?

» *Dissolution*—What happens if, for example, you are forced to declare bankruptcy and liquidate the company's assets?

» *Disassociation*—What happens if one partner decides to take early retirement, or if you and your partner have an irreconcilable conflict and no longer want to work together? Who gets what?

These scenarios demand calm, reasoned thinking, which can be hard to come by when emotions are high. This is similar to the need for advance directives in healthcare. Many couples set up these legal instruments so that in the future, should one partner become seriously ill and unable to communicate—for example, fall into a coma after a stroke—that partner's wishes for extraordinary care are already known and legally acknowledged. Advance directives allow families to avoid emotional, irrational fights over who gets to make life-or-death decisions by putting those decisions on paper twenty-five years before they're needed.

Preparation in business does the same thing. It protects you, your partners, and your family in the event of a sudden death or disability or an emotionally charged event like a divorce or the breakup of a partnership. By preparing the proper legal documents with the help of an experienced attorney, you're taking emotions out of the equation and creating mechanisms to maintain business continuity in the event of an unexpected crisis. You may never need these measures, but like health, fire, and auto insurance, it's essential to have them in place. Because the unexpected happens.

THE SECRET

If your business is a C or an S corporation, work with your attorney to set up a business continuity agreement, which is also known as a buy-sell agreement. (If you're set up as an LLC, then these protections should be part of your operating agreement.)

Basically, a buy-sell agreement controls the transfer of ownership in a business when certain events occur. It's an arm's-length contract, which means that it is not required by law. However, it is one of the most sensible pieces of legal protection that business owners can put in place and worth every penny of the legal fees. Depending on how you choose to construct it, a buy-sell agreement requires certain activity should one or more of the following events occur:

» Sudden death of a business partner

» Disability of a partner

» Divorce of a partner

» Early retirement of a partner

» Termination of a partner

» Bankruptcy

» Abrupt closure of the business

» Mutual dissolution of the partner relationship

» Unresolvable conflict between business partners

If and when the unexpected happens, the buy-sell agreement may set out a number of guidelines, such as the following:

» Requiring that the corporation or the remaining owners buy the exiting, disabled, or deceased owner's stock

» Giving the corporation or the remaining owners the first option to purchase the stock from the exiting owner or the owner's estate

» Requiring that an heir, an ex-spouse, or any other party who could be in a position to receive a departed owner's shares sell those shares to the other owner(s)

» Establishing a formula for determining the value of the shares—for example, a multiple of earnings. You can also do this with an appraiser, but that is more costly and can result in conflict when both the corporation and the exiting partner (or his or her estate) hire competing appraisers.

With a buy-sell agreement, ownership in the business can be transferred only according to the rules put in place within the agreement. The agreement ensures that the business is valued properly for all parties, and it prevents remaining or surviving partners from being forced to become business partners with their partner's spouse or children. The agreement also fixes your company's valuation for estate tax purposes. If you haven't fixed the value of your business at death, the IRS can use a variety of valuation methods in order to determine the value of your estate, and those methods may increase the tax that your heirs owe. A properly drafted buy-sell agreement avoids this interference by setting that value.

An agreement can also be used to fix the terms and conditions of any transfer of stock, including interest rate, length of buyout period, and security. In other words, it establishes a market for part or all of the company's shares at an agreed-upon price. Should an unexpected event occur, the involved parties can avoid expensive, time-consuming legal battles and the business can continue to operate smoothly and profitably.

There are two main types of buy-sell agreements:

1. *Cross-purchase*—The cross-purchase agreement allows the remaining owners of a business to purchase the shares of an owner upon a triggering event like death, disability, or retirement. It also requires that the departing owner or his estate sell the shares if the partners choose to exercise this option. To fund the purchase, each owner must take out an

insurance policy on the other owners, listing him- or herself as the beneficiary. If one of the owners dies or leaves, the combined funds from the insurance policies can be used to purchase the deceased owner's interest.

› Advantages: The remaining owners receive a step-up in basis equal to the price of the shares purchased. That can mean lower capital gains taxes down the road than with the stock redemption option (which I'll describe next).

› Disadvantages: You and the other owners could wind up taking out several insurance policies on each owner if there are more than two partners.

2. *Stock redemption*—In this case, the corporation buys an insurance policy on each owner. The corporation is the premium payer, owner, and beneficiary. Each owner becomes the insured.

› Advantages: Only one insurance policy is required per business owner, reducing costs.

› Disadvantages: There is no step-up in basis upon the death or departure of the owner. So each remaining owner's business interest increases, but he or she will also owe more capital gains taxes down the road when it comes time to sell.

Regardless of the type, your buy-sell agreement should cover a couple of other common contingencies:

» *Bankruptcy/divorce*—If an owner files for bankruptcy or is involved in a divorce, he or she can be forced to transfer ownership to a creditor or a former spouse. The agreement should give the business the opportunity to acquire the owner's stock in the event that one of these involuntary transfers is on the horizon.

» *Restrictions on transferring stock to non-owners*—If an owner is considering offering his or her shares to an outside party, the agreement would require him or her to first offer to sell the shares back to the company or to the remaining co-owners at the same price and terms offered to the would-be outside buyer. If the share price set down in the agreement and the price offered to the would-be buyer are different, the remaining co-owners pay the lower of the two.

As I mentioned above, buy-sell agreements generally require the owners of a business to take out an insurance policy whose benefit will be used to cover the cost of buying the shares of an owner who has died, been disabled, or left the business for some reason. When the death of an owner is the main concern, a life insurance policy is the primary need. However, there are other types of insurance that should also be considered:

» *Disability buyout (DB) insurance*—Don't confuse this with disability income (DI) insurance. DI normally pays a percentage of the disabled owner's regular monthly earnings until he overcomes the disability or reaches a certain age, such as sixty-five. Disability buyout insurance, on the other hand, is paid to the business (or the other owner) in a lump sum or as a series of payments over several years, with the intention of buying out the disabled owner's stock. DB won't cover more than 80 percent of the buyout price, so there will still be a balance owed. It's important to agree in advance to the payment terms (length of time, interest rate, etc.) on the portion owed and to include them in the buy-sell agreement.

» *Key person insurance*—This is an insurance policy that can be bought for owners or even critical employees based on their value to the company. A key person policy is valuable because it can fund the purchase of an ownership share when it follows a noncatastrophic event—that is, not death or disability but early retirement or the breakdown of a co-owner relationship.

Let's say that Adam and Bob go into business together and they're doing great. A couple of years later, Bob dies. Without an agreement, Bob's ownership interest passes to his heirs, either by law or according to his will. All of a sudden, Adam has new partners whom he can't stand and who know and care nothing about the business. What can Adam do to mitigate those effects?

Fortunately, these partners were smart. They set up a buy-sell agreement when the business launched, and it gives Adam the right to buy the deceased partner's shares, which are held in trust by his estate. Bob's widow has no choice in the matter; she must sell the shares to Bob, the remaining owner. The sale price is based on a formula both partners agreed to: five times earnings.

But there's a hiccup. According to the five-times-earnings formula, the fair market value of Bob's shares is $2.5 million. Adam doesn't have $2.5 million in cash. That's where the life insurance policy comes in. The policy pays a benefit of $2 million, which is used to buy the majority of the shares, and the buy-sell agreement gives Adam the right to pay off the $500,000 balance over ten years at a modest interest rate. The surviving partner gains sole control of the company, while the heirs of the deceased owner get the cash.

Your business continuity agreement is likely the most important document you can have as a business owner. Don't neglect it because you think the worst can't happen. It *does* happen, every day—to people who never thought it would happen to them either.

HOW YOU'LL BENEFIT

The greatest benefit of planning for the unexpected is that it ensures that unforeseeable events will not prevent your business from continuing to operate. A buy-sell agreement enables the remaining owners to quickly acquire the remaining ownership interest and move on without incurring undue legal costs and spending lots of time in court. But planning ahead also helps to prevent the kinds of conflicts that can, at best, make life miserable and, at worst, damage your business.

The other key benefit of the buy-sell agreement and related insurance is that these measures can prevent or minimize personal conflict. One of the realities most commonly ignored by entrepreneurs, especially when starting their business, is that life happens. People change. Conditions change.

"Clients say, 'I don't need this agreement because my partner is my brother, and we're not going to get in a fight,'" says Mike Tucci, a Cleveland-based attorney specializing in corporate and intellectual property law.[21] Tucci continues:

> I try to contain my laughter. Nobody is more likely to fight than brothers. I'll reply, "That's great, but what if your brother becomes chronically ill in five years?" People who are starting a business tend to be upbeat and

positive that they are going to succeed, but that's the time when they can easily gloss over the fact that things happen in life.

It's the job of the lawyers to say, "Look, I'm not saying that these things will happen, but it's my job to prepare you for what *might* happen." Buy-sell agreements are preventive maintenance. If you don't prepare, then you're going to court, spending money, and acting on emotion. The costs involved are a down payment on a smoother transition when something happens that breaks up your partnership.

As Tucci points out, agreements bring order and predictability to some of the most chaotic situations a business owner can face. For example, the meaning of *death* is pretty clear, but how do you define *disability*? Must an owner be unable to perform his duties for ninety days to be legally disabled? Or does it take the opinions of two physicians? In your buy-sell agreement, you can define precisely what triggers an automatic stock sale.

Divorce is inherently chaotic, but suddenly having a partner's ex-spouse as co-owner of your business is a potential nightmare. Mandating the sale of the divorcing partner's stock in your agreement avoids this stressful situation. And after all, the ex-spouse would probably rather have cash than a share of the company anyway.

In the unhappy event that you dissolve your company due to litigation or some other problem, your buy-sell agreement firmly sets the "who gets what" terms in advance. Once you follow the law and pay your creditors, you and your partners divide up the remaining assets according to whatever you deem fair. But who decides what's fair? You could divide things according to each person's percentage of ownership, but that doesn't help with assets like machinery. Setting down the specifics of a liquidation in your agreement helps avoid problems.

As Tucci reveals, disassociation can take many forms:

One is where an owner says, "I want to get out of the business, and my friend Joe wants to buy me out." Well, what if you, the remaining owner, think Joe is a crook? The only way to control your ownership interest is by creating an agreement and putting certain limitations in it. For example, you can stipulate that you get right of first refusal if your business partner wants to sell his shares to an outsider.

Another issue comes when there are fifty-fifty partners. "Suppose there's a stalemate over a major decision. One partner says, "Screw you, I'm leaving, and you can buy me out." The other partner says, "No, I'm leaving, and *you* can buy *me* out." How do you resolve this? They could agree to sell, but there may be no buyer. In that case, deadlock resolution mechanisms come into play. These have colorful names like "Texas shoot-out" and "Russian roulette," and ultimately they decide who stays and who goes. You can specify your deadlock resolution methods in your agreement.

A business partnership can end for many reasons. What if one owner has to relocate to look after a sick relative? What if your business partner is prosecuted for a crime and sent to jail? You can't address every possible contingency, but you can put yourself and your business in the best possible position to weather the storms that do come.

WHAT TO DO

If your business has more than one owner, consult an attorney specializing in corporate law about setting up a buy-sell agreement. Don't make assumptions or delay. Death, disability, or some other calamity can hit without any warning. Get good advice from a good lawyer, and follow it. Consider it a kind of "future insurance."

EXIT 911 What if you're already facing the death of a business partner or an impending divorce, and you don't have a buy-sell agreement in place? Head for your lawyer's office. There may be steps you can take that will prevent an ugly confrontation with heirs or an ex-spouse, including mediation, binding arbitration, and deadlock resolution.

Did You Know . . . ?

Having a tax or business attorney set up your buy-sell agreement will typically cost between $2,500 and $5,000. That's a small price to pay for a document that might prevent ownership conflicts from destroying your business during a crisis.

DON'T BET YOUR RETIREMENT ON STARTING ANOTHER SUCCESSFUL BUSINESS

Once you begin to believe that you are infallible, that success will automatically lead to more success, and that you have "got it made," reality will be sure to give you a rude wake-up call.
—FELIX DENNIS, ENTREPRENEUR AND AUTHOR OF HOW TO GET RICH

THE FACTS

After the years of sweat, blood, and tears you've put into your business, the thing you may find most difficult is being out of it. When it comes to the personal challenges that most business owners face after an exit, the Columbia Business School white paper *Life After an Exit: How Entrepreneurs Transition to the Next Stage* says it all:

> Most entrepreneurs do not measure success in terms of financial rewards, but rather by the sense of freedom and potential legacy that these financial rewards confer. Entrepreneurs often struggle with how best to use their new freedom and how to define their legacy. Some engage in philanthropy and government service, while others develop personal interests, or pursue new learnings and startup ventures. However, finding the next fulfilling activity is one of the key challenges that all entrepreneurs face after a sale.[22]

In other words, it's hard to be out of the game. That's why many entrepreneurs who work hard to reach their liquidity events wind up starting new ventures not long after selling. Once they've spent a few years traveling, renovating the house, playing golf, and maybe training for a marathon, they find they don't know what to do with themselves if they're not trying to build a company from the ground up.

This is especially true in the technology sector, where there's a long-standing tradition of young moguls making their millions and bolting before age thirty-five. For example, Marc Andreessen, one of the creators of Netscape Navigator, the first widely popular web browser, became a billionaire when Netscape sold to America Online in 1998 for $4.2 billion. Within a year, he left the company to launch Loudcloud, and over the next nine years he invested in forty-five startup companies, including Twitter.[23]

But even older business owners who might retire at the traditional retirement age can become restless and unhappy when they trade the daily challenges of running a company for the supposed pleasures of gardening and reading. And it's not just the ex-entrepreneurs who suffer—their families also feel the effects of this major life change. At the end of a widely circulated joke about a woman whose recently retired husband hangs around the house and doesn't know what to do with himself, the exasperated wife finally shouts, "I married you for better or for worse, but not for lunch!"

Faced with idleness, boredom, and the hunger for new challenges, some former business owners invest substantial portions of the money from their liquidity events in new business ventures. Wealth preservation strategies become of paramount importance here. Entrepreneurs who are feeling depressed, lonely, and disconnected can become irrational and sink too much of their sale proceeds into their startups. That's bad enough if you're forty and you were counting on the money to finance your next career rehabbing and flipping condos. It's potentially catastrophic if you're sixty-five and you need the funds from your sale to live on for the rest of your life.

In my experience, the older the entrepreneur at the time of his or her exit, the less likely he or she is to crave the dopamine rush that comes with starting a new company. Somebody over fifty-five years old who's been running his kitchen renovation company since he was thirty probably feels as though he has a lot of life left unlived. He wants to spend more time with his spouse, kids, or grandchildren. He has a backlog of books to read and places to visit. And he probably still has the physical vitality to try things like hiking the Appalachian Trail or training for an Ironman competition. If he invests wisely, he'll spend the next twenty years too busy to even think about business.

The woman who launches an Internet company at age thirty and sells it at thirty-five is a different story. She doesn't see her exit as an ending, but as the close of one chapter of her career and the gateway to the next chapter. It's a near-certainty that she'll start at least one more business, maybe several. The big difference between the young serial entrepreneur and the older one is obvious: When you're thirty-five and you burn 75 percent of the proceeds from the sale of your business on a startup, you have time to recover. When you're sixty, you don't. But even at thirty-five, would you want to consume most of your liquidity event proceeds, considering that your next venture probably won't be as successful?

In any case, launching a new business isn't really the problem. Entrepreneurs are driven to build and create, and starting a venture that lets you do both can be a healthy, productive way to occupy your post-work life. The problem is the *I'll just start another multimillion-dollar success* mind-set. It's dangerous for two reasons:

1. The odds of lightning striking twice—an entrepreneur launching a successful new company on the heels of his or her last one—are very long. It's very common that the post-exit startup is a failure.

2. Because they are coming off a successful exit, some entrepreneurs believe they are bulletproof, so they invest far more of their nest egg than they should in their new venture. If it fails, they can wind up without enough money to last the rest of their lives.

As Roman Stanek, founder and CEO of GoodData, said in an interview on www.businessinsider.com, "The second company is harder. Most people fail at their second companies because they believe they have the magic formula. They think, 'I will only fix the problems of the first company, and the second company will run like it's on autopilot.' But the problem is that the environment is always different."[24]

Nobody is immune—not even people with a string of successes. Kamran Elahian, a so-called serial entrepreneur who was involved in such successful pre-dotcom startups as CAE Systems, Cirrus Logic, Centillium Communications, and NeoMagic, saw several ventures bomb. After CAE Systems sold to Tektronix in 1983 for $75 million, Elahian started Momenta Corporation, which developed the presumptive next big thing: pen computers. Whoops. Pen computers tanked, and in 1992 so did Momenta, to the tune of $40 million in venture capital lost and $18 million more in debt.[25]

For someone who has hundreds of millions of dollars burning a hole in the proverbial pocket, having a new venture lose $40 million is distressing, but it's not a personal disaster. Most business owners don't have that luxury. If you sold your business for $10 million and netted $7 million after capital gains taxes, commissions, and other expenses, you may need most or all of that money to live on in retirement.

There are a few more potential red flags involved in starting a new company after a business exit:

» You may be prohibited by a noncompete agreement from working in the industry you just left. So two years after selling your gourmet coffee roasting company, you're dying to get back into the coffee business, but you can't. You signed a five-year noncompete. You can't work in the industry or reach out to your old business contacts. You have to begin all over again in another industry. Imagine starting a new company at fifty-five years old in a niche where you're a novice.

» Investing in a startup is basically investing in a single micro-cap stock. Imagine someone receiving $10 million from a liquidity event and then taking $4 million and buying one micro-cap stock. Considering that about 80 percent of new businesses are doomed to failure, you would think that person was insane, wouldn't you? That's basically what you're doing when you invest in a private startup. No matter how successful you've been in the past, it's a huge gamble.

THE SECRET

Establish a "bucket" system for using the money from your sale. If you suspect that the entrepreneurial bug will bite you after you've exited your current business, planning ahead for how you'll use the money will keep you from becoming your own worst enemy. Hire a financial advisor to help you create your financial plan, and long before you begin the exit process, share the secret of your bucket system. This could mean the difference between using your money wisely and spending like a fool.

The bucket system works like this:

» *Nest egg bucket*—Between 50 and 90 percent of the funds you get from your liquidity event go into this bucket. The amount depends on what you and your advisor have determined you need to live on in retirement. Generally, the smaller the liquidity event, the bigger chunk of the sale funds that need to go into this bucket. Once they're in, it's hands off for any business purposes. This money is for living expenses, from travel to healthcare.

» *Risky venture bucket*—The rest of your money goes here, and it's yours to use on new business ventures. This is the money you're free to risk on that single micro-cap stock you call "my new company."

The catch is that you can't dip into your nest egg bucket to keep your new venture running. Once you've burnt through the risky venture bucket, the nest egg bucket is off limits. This is why it's so important to have a trusted financial advisor on your team. Entrepreneurs sometimes have this sense that they are invincible and that every business they touch will turn to gold. More than once, I've had clients come to me after selling one company and starting another and ask me for funds from their nest egg bucket to dump into their struggling new venture. It's my duty to advise them against tapping those funds.

Those are not easy conversations to have, because people's egos are on the line. If they press me, however, I remind them of the plan we've made and the effect that losing another million dollars or so will have on their retirement. Even the most stubborn entrepreneur sobers up when you tell him that he might have to get a job when he's eighty years old.

David Reske did it right. In 1994 he started his first company, web development and Internet marketing firm Onward Technologies. In 1998, when he was thirty-six, he sold the company to Computer Sciences Corporation for an undisclosed sum, and in 1999 he left to start Nowspeed. "I had a vision for how people could use mobile devices to access their email," he says. "Unfortunately, I was a little ahead of my time."[26]

Nowspeed struggled, and David shut it down in 2002. But he did so without damaging his family's finances. He began with a goal of putting 10 percent of the value of his liquidity event into the venture and ended up investing 20 percent—not the best outcome, but not catastrophic. "I wasn't willing to recommit any more money," he says. "The liquidity event was good for my family."

The shutdown allowed David to regroup, and in 2003 he used the Nowspeed corporate shell to relaunch the company in an area he already knew: Internet marketing. Nowspeed now has fifteen employees; focuses on website design, search engine optimization, and online advertising; and typically works with retainer clients, which means more stable revenues.

"I was surprised at how hard it was to start again from scratch," David says. "You get used to having a good management team, and now you have to make your own sales calls again. I was going into a different industry, and I had lot to learn." His advice for the successful ex–business owner looking to scratch the entrepreneurial itch:

Decide what to do with your liquidity event before you sell. You don't want to sell and then have to work again. If you do have to work, do you really want to sell? Also, limit the amount of your liquidity event that gets invested into your next venture, and don't underestimate the cost and effort that will go into that venture.

You're an entrepreneur by nature, so it stands to reason that you can barely contain your instinct to start up a new venture. The two-bucket system is an asset allocation strategy that is designed to help protect you from yourself. This simple approach could prevent you from suffering the catastrophic loss of your new-found wealth.

HOW YOU'LL BENEFIT

You can think about limiting your potential post-exit business losses in the same way that you think about building a portfolio of retirement investments in an SEP or a 401(k) account. The conventional wisdom suggests that as you get older, your investments should become less risky because you have less time to recover losses. A time-tested financial planning adage is the Rule of One

Hundred: Take 100 minus your age, and that's the percentage of your portfolio that should be in stocks. So a forty-year-old might have 60 percent (100 minus 40) of his 401(k) assets invested in various stock funds (blue chip, midcap, and so on). But a seventy-year-old should invest only about 30 percent (100 minus 70) of his money in stocks. The rest should be in less volatile investments such as US Treasury bonds. The return will be lower, but the need to preserve capital is greater.

Limiting your potential exposure to losses related to a business startup has the same benefit: It preserves more of your capital. Given life expectancies today, if you sell your company tomorrow at age fifty-five and you're in good health, you can reasonably expect to live another thirty-five to forty years. Odds are, your money will last for the rest of your and your spouse's lives only if you invest prudently, and that includes keeping a tight rein on the amount you're willing to invest in any new venture.

You might have no interest whatsoever in starting a new company after you leave the one you're running now. That's great, but that's today. Believe me, I've seen more than one former business owner change that tune after a few months of waking up in the morning with no place to go. You know those professional athletes who couldn't seem to give up the game, like basketball's Michael Jordan and baseball's Rickey Henderson? Each time they retired, I'll bet they swore to themselves that this time it was for good. But they couldn't stay away.

You don't know how you'll feel after you leave your business. Determining right now the amount of your sale proceeds you can allocate toward your risky venture bucket can save you a lot of grief later on.

WHAT TO DO

1. *Have the "What's next?" talk.* According to Columbia Business School, "Financial analysis and planning before and immediately after a sale of a venture is crucial. In the most successful transitions, entrepreneurs sought out professional advice in a variety of financial areas, including tax, philanthropy, estate planning, and wealth education for children, well in advance of the sale."[27] Sit down with your financial advisor and talk about what you might want to do after your exit. Speculate on possible new businesses you might start. What would the likely startup costs be? Would you self-fund or seek venture or angel funding?

2. *Run your plan.* Using conservative projections of what your company might sell for when you're ready to exit and the best estimate of the funds you and your family will need to live on, project your financial plan based on losing the money that you might invest in a new business. What happens if you reinvest 20 percent of your liquidity event value and lose

it? Does your financial plan still work? What if you lose 30 percent? Project the impact of various investments and various losses until you reach a tolerable loss percentage at which your money will still last for the rest of your life. That's the threshold you cannot cross.

3. *Give your advisor veto power.* Even an advisor who's working under the legal fiduciary standard can't withhold your money from you. But if you give your advisor permission to make it as hard as possible for you to tap your nest egg for more business capital, you'll be doing yourself a favor. Work out the dynamic ahead of time to avoid conflict in the heat of the moment.

4. *Start small.* Let's say that after your liquidity event, you find the idea of launching a new company irresistible. Who says you have to spend $2 million on a startup? Most entrepreneurs start their first businesses with little or no capital. They set up offices in their homes, garages, or basements. They hire people who will work for stock options. They put in long hours and find innovative ways to save. Why not bootstrap your second venture? Cash flow, lines of credit, and/or the cash pool of a liquidity event can spoil many entrepreneurs; they come to believe that to start something, you have to spend, spend, spend. You don't. Think small. After all, it worked for you the first time.

5. *Buy into an existing business.* Another option for the ex-owner with an itchy trigger finger is to buy a share of an existing company. This has many advantages, including no startup costs and an established customer base and business model. Of course, there's a big disadvantage: You're not going to be the head honcho. For people used to running the show, that can be a deal breaker. If buying into another company does appeal to you, though, be sure to do your due diligence. You don't want to invest in a business with shaky management or a technology niche that's becoming obsolete.

6. *Buy into a franchise.* Becoming an owner-operator of a franchised business is another way to get back in action while keeping your risk to a minimum. The obvious advantage is that this business model has already been battle-tested and is proven to be profitable. Many of the country's most successful companies, such as the Subway sandwich chain, are built on franchisees. Startup costs can be considerable: in the hundreds of thousands of dollars for something like a 7-Eleven store, and more than $1 million for a McDonald's franchise. But if you would be likely to invest the same amount in a startup anyway, a franchise could be a much lower-risk way to satisfy your desire to stay in the game. There's a reason that there are more than 800,000 franchised businesses in

the United States, which together contribute more than $2 trillion to the country's economy.[28]

7. *Consult.* Consulting lets you leverage your expertise and remain active in your field while spending only as much as it takes to create a website and print up business cards. Work with companies in your niche, use your expertise to help them be more successful, and earn a healthy per-project income. Of course, it's possible that a noncompete clause in the sale agreement for your existing company might prevent you from doing this. But if you know going into a sale that you'd like to transition into consulting work, you could always negotiate a noncompete that would prevent you only from *starting* your own company.

You might not be able to anticipate your desire to continue working after your liquidity event, even in a limited capacity. Plenty of entrepreneurs don't know how much they'll miss being in the game until they leave the locker room. So have the conversation now. Create your plan. Think about possible post-work business options, and cross off the ones that don't appeal to you. Run the numbers. Luck favors the prepared.

EXIT 911 Assuming you're still running your business, there isn't much chance of an emergency popping up here. If you're about a year out from your desired exit, sit down with your financial advisor and discuss possible loss scenarios based on the likely size of your liquidity event and your anticipated living expenses in retirement. If you're younger and you have no intention of retiring after selling your company, then talk about your goals for the money you'll make in a sale. Do you want to pay off your house? Create a trust for your kids? Buy a Ferrari? Or just take a two-year vacation before diving into your next venture? Your risk tolerance will depend on your age and goals. Set up your plan before you get into the exit process—and stick to it.

Did You Know . . . ?

Selling your business is always cause for celebration, right? Well, it may not be as simple as that, according to a survey by accounting firm Rothstein Kass. The poll of 116 ex-owners of small to midmarket businesses found that 54 percent were dissatisfied with the process of selling their companies. The former owners claimed two main reasons for their seller's remorse: (1) Their exit advisors did not work as a team; and (2) their advisors were unresponsive. It is interesting that while only 8 percent of respondents were dissatisfied with their sale price, 30 percent were unhappy with the personal wealth they gained from the sale. That suggests a lack of advance financial planning. The solution, according to the survey? Extensive pre-exit corporate and personal financial planning.[29]

FIND SOMETHING TO FILL THE VOID AFTER YOUR LIQUIDITY EVENT

It's good to have money and the things that money can buy,
but it's good, too, to check up once in a while and make sure
that you haven't lost the things that money can't buy.
—*GEORGE LORIMER, JOURNALIST AND EDITOR*

THE FACTS

You've built your company from nothing with blood, sweat, and sacrifice. You've put everything of yourself into it. It's your baby. It's your life's work. For years, your life may have centered on being the owner of your business. Do you really think it will be easy to walk away from all that?

It won't be. It never is, even for people who are looking forward to retirement.

Many business owners fail to consider how they will feel when they are no longer involved in their companies. But as I mentioned in the previous secret, just take a look at longtime professional athletes who retire after twenty years in their sports—Michael Jordan, Rickey Henderson, Brett Favre. Sure, they're leaving behind the endless training, travel, and injuries. But they are also leaving behind the thing that defines them, and often that departure leaves them emotionally lost and spiritually devastated. Or think about people who have lived their lives in a northern climate and always dreamed of retiring and moving south. Once they move, however, they find out that although the weather is better, they miss their friends, family, hobbies, what have you, and they move back home to reclaim their lost identity.

Emotional baggage can even jeopardize the sale of your company. Jeff Spadafora is the director of Global Coaching & Product Development for Halftime, a firm that helps people in midlife—often former business owners—find meaningful ways to use their time and wealth. He told me a story of a business owner who wanted to sell his small business. His exit planner did a valuation and came up with an open market value of $4 million. "They put the company on the market to see if anybody was interested in buying it and instantly got two buyers offering the full $4 million value," says Jeff. "Over the next nine days, the thing escalated into a bidding war. The bids went from $4 million to $6 million to $9 million to $11 million!"[30]

The owner was thrilled at the prospect of getting nearly three times his asking price for his company, right? Wrong. "The owner disappeared," Jeff says. "Literally disappeared. I don't mean like he had been really busy and hard to reach. I mean he had family and friends who had no idea where he was and were *this close* to calling the FBI. Then out of nowhere the guy emerges and tells the exit planner to call the deal off."

Why did the owner scuttle what could have been the deal of a lifetime? Jeff says he told his exit planner, "I don't know what I'd do with myself without my business." He'd hit the jackpot, but no amount of money would have helped with the pain of the separation from what he had built. The sale collapsed.

That's an extreme example, but emotional attachment to a business can cause all sorts of problems for its owner. Sorrow, anger, and depression can become real issues that impact the owner's liquidity event and make life miserable afterward. Imagine it: One day you're getting more than two hundred emails a day, and the next day you're emailing yourself to make sure your email still works! That's not a joke; I've seen it happen. You're used to being the head honcho, and suddenly no one is coming to you asking you to make big decisions or solve problems. It's a blow to the ego and to your sense of purpose. Without your company to work on, what will you do with your time? Why do you matter?

Jeff explains:

One of the biggest challenges business owners face is this sense that they're losing their identity. When you stay focused on building a business over a long period of time, and give a lot of emotional energy to that endeavor, you start to identify yourself as the founder and CEO. When you sell that business, it's literally like your identity has been handed over to someone else. You need to figure out, *Who am I without my business card?* Not everyone has a good answer.

Entrepreneurs who don't have that answer can damage their post-work lives with poor choices, such as the following:

» *Starting a new venture out of desperation.* As I discussed earlier, having one company succeed is no guarantee that a second company will survive the startup process. Over-investing in a new company is a risky move that can imperil your retirement. Some entrepreneurs will start philanthropic ventures with the best of intentions, not realizing that a nonprofit can still eat up all your time and money. Jeff from Halftime has seen this scenario play out on many occasions:

People will dive into starting a new organization, but they can't let go of their old do-it-yourself mind-set. I was working with a guy who sold the second-largest helicopter medevac company in America and spent some time working to help kids with autism because his daughter was autistic. But he didn't partner with anyone who actually knew about the new therapies for autism. He thought he was too smart for partnering; he had always been the CEO, not a team player. So he spent a ton of money coming up with this therapy camp for autistic kids, and it failed.

This guy hadn't failed at anything in about thirty years, and he had a year of total failure. His wife was incredibly irritated with him; she just wanted some time with her husband and for both of them to "detox." But after his attempt at doing something altruistic failed, the guy bought his former competitor in the helicopter business. Unbelievable.

» *Yielding to addictive behavior.* David J. Linden, professor of neuroscience at Johns Hopkins University School of Medicine, says that entrepreneurs and other leaders are compulsive risk takers who seek the intense stimulation of novelty, a behavior they share with people who are addicted to gambling, alcohol, sex, or drugs.[31] Some entrepreneurs, unable to replicate the high of running a successful business in a world of tough competitors, might turn to potentially addictive activities in order to get the same dopamine rush they once got from closing a big deal.

» *Remaining involved with the old company.* Whether at the insistence of the buyer or at their own request, some business owners remain involved with their companies for a certain term after the sale. However, a few stay on even after fulfilling their contractual obligation because they can't let go, and those experiences are rarely satisfying. Think about it: It's no longer your company. The systems and procedures you put in place may change. The culture often shifts radically as the acquiring company moves toward an emphasis on yearly earnings. You're just another cog instead of the person at the wheel.

Even if you don't go to such extremes, failing to recognize and deal with your own complex emotions about selling your company could lessen your enjoyment of the post-work life you've worked so long and hard to achieve.

THE SECRET

Deal with the emotions involved in walking away from your business long before you try to sell. Too many entrepreneurs ignore those feelings and wind up either sabotaging their exit or experiencing levels of stress or grief that can interfere with post-work life. Instead of trying to tough it out, it may be time to reframe the issue.

Historically, entrepreneurs are problem solvers. Your formula for success is straightforward: Collect information, make plans, and when you're ready, pull the trigger on a decision. However, that formula probably won't work in the season of life when you're trying to figure out why you're on this earth—how you can give back, how you can bring meaning and purpose to your life, and so on. That's a journey, not a decision. It requires a new approach and new questions.

In working with its clients, Halftime recommends beginning the journey by dividing it into three issues that entrepreneurs need to address in the "second half" of life:

1. *Core.* Who are you? What are you passionate about? What are you good at? What are you not good at? How do you want to spend your time? These are questions that speak to your core—the center of who you are.

   "The question of time is very common," says Jeff Spadafora. "About a year after selling his company, a client said to me, 'I got my golf handicap down from a twelve to a seven, but I'm just not that interested in getting it down to five. I want to do something, make a difference in the world, but I just don't have a clue where to start.'"

2. *Capacity.* There are three main areas that make up this category. *Time* is the first: How much time can you dedicate to whatever you decide to do in your post-work life? Do you want to make charity a full-time job? Or do you want to devote time to a "passion project," such as mentoring young entrepreneurs? Or do you plan to focus on getting back in touch with family and friends? Many entrepreneurs sacrifice their personal relationships when they start their companies; some of the time after your liquidity event should go toward rekindling those relationships, especially with your spouse.

"There's a lot of collateral damage around an entrepreneur's singular focus on his or her business," Jeff says. "Some guys talk about spending their time playing golf, sailing, and traveling around the world after they sell. And some need to do that so they can relax and reconnect with their spouse."

Money is also a capacity. How much do you need to live on? How much do you want to put into your charitable foundation or passion project? What about college savings for your kids, if you're at that life stage? You should be working with your financial advisor to answer those questions.

The third capacity is what Jeff calls *spiritual overflow*:

> Guys at this stage of life get pretty existential. They've sold their business, they have an empty nest and a pile of cash, and they bump up against

their purpose. They start asking tough questions: *Where does God fit into this? Is there a God?* Moving into a life of service and sacrifice costs energy, and many people need to refill their tanks with spiritual overflow.

3. *Context.* Context is about grasping the things you don't know and understanding how other parties may bring to the table skills or resources that you lack. Do you partner with an organization to pursue your passionate cause? Do you start something of your own? CEOs and entrepreneurs tend to be lone wolves who try to come up with the answers themselves. But being an expert in software development doesn't make you an expert in childhood literacy. For many former chief executives, admitting their ignorance about a subject is the first step to teaming with great people.

Another wrinkle, says Jeff, is that while many entrepreneurs find that their business gets in the way of the life they want to live, some see it as the perfect platform for creating the ideal post-work life. "When that happens," he says, "they will stop the exit process. They will change the paradigm of the business and repurpose it to serve what they want and the meaning in their lives." A business built around your larger life—instead of the other way around—can become a source of cash, resources, and inspiration to do what brings you fulfillment.

The post-work stage of life should be about going from *success* to *significance*—that is, going from focusing on your own achievements, money, and accolades to focusing on what you're truly passionate about, such as serving other individuals, your community, and humanity. It makes sense that many people refer to this interval as "halftime," a period of pause like the break in a football or basketball game: During this time, you have the good fortune to stop, regroup, rest from your labors, and decide the shape that the next stage of your life will take. If you choose, you can reinvent yourself for the "second half" of your life. The entrepreneurs I've worked with who've gotten the most satisfaction out of the post-exit phase of their lives have been the ones who invest not just in their finances but in their physical health, their relationships, and their sense of purpose.

A quote most often attributed to management consultant Peter Drucker says, "People are over-prepared for Life One and under-prepared for Life Two, and there's no university for Life Two." Before you plan your exit, take the time to prepare for your "new" life.

HOW YOU'LL BENEFIT

Facing and dealing with any uncomfortable emotions regarding the sale of your business will benefit you personally, of course, as will finding ways to serve your passions after your exit. Whether they spend more time with their grandchildren, volunteer, or take up something like art or music, the entrepreneurs who find ways to express their passions tend to transition into the most successful post-exit lifestyles. But let's step away from the personal for a moment and talk about the financial benefits of embracing "halftime."

Choosing satisfying, challenging new ways to spend your time and money can make for a smoother, faster sale process. An owner who seems erratic or ambivalent about selling can scare buyers away; no one wants to spend time and money doing due diligence and writing offers only to have the seller back out at the eleventh hour because of emotional concerns. If you enter your exit period free of nagging doubts about selling your company, you're more likely to proceed with confidence and consistency, which are reassuring to potential buyers.

When you are keeping busy and you feel fulfilled, you're also more likely to make wise post-exit investments. People who find themselves facing a black hole of purposeless time after selling their business wind up blowing this chance for a "second life"; they dump money into an ill-advised new business because they can't stand being at home anymore, buy risky stocks for the financial thrill ride, or become angel investors to get a vicarious startup buzz. Those are effective ways to burn up a large chunk of the money you need to live on after your exit. Nobody should be so desperate to recapture the excitement of running a business that they're forced to get a new job at age seventy.

One of the benefits of financial stability can be relationship stability. Contrary to popular belief, there's no statistical evidence to support the idea that entrepreneurs have a higher divorce rate than the general population. But it's safe to say that anything that leads to relationship neglect can lead to instability and costly breakups. Years of preoccupation with your business may begin to cause rifts in marriage and family, so use an upcoming exit as a chance to reconnect and give more time to your spouse, children, and friends. It's not money but *people* who give meaning to our lives, and science shows us that people with stronger, closer social circles also tend to enjoy lives that are longer and healthier.

WHAT TO DO

Prepare yourself for your eventual exit. Ask the questions now about how you'll spend your time and how you'll define yourself when you no longer have to get up every morning to run your company. The sooner you start thinking about it, the sooner you can make purpose and meaning part of your comprehensive exit strategy.

Here is some advice to get you started:

1. *Ask the unasked questions.* If you've spent the last twenty years sinking every thought into making your company successful, you've probably ignored the bigger questions of life. When you're thinking about your exit, it's time to start asking those

questions. What do you care about? What things have you always wanted to do but never done because there was no time? What kind of legacy would you like to leave? What could you do for your family? What does your perfect post-work life look like?

2. *Update your personal financial plan.* Consider whether you want to set up a charitable trust or foundation. Review your estate planning. If an offer is on the table, do your due diligence on any earn-outs and make sure you're realistic about the money you're likely to receive. List your post-work expenses, paying special attention to healthcare, which costs more as you age. Figure out how much you will need in order to live the lifestyle you desire.

3. *Set specific post-work goals.* Discuss with your spouse and your financial advisor the things you'd like to do after you exit. Are you dying to spend a year traveling around the world? Great. But what comes after that? If you would like to help out the university where you got your master's degree, how will you do that and how much will it cost? How many days per week will you dedicate to passion projects? When you're in the middle of selling your business, having a precise plan will help you transition seamlessly to the next phase.

4. *Have your exit team in place.* Apart from all the sound financial and legal reasons for this, it's important to hand the reins

to people who can execute the details of your exit impartially and without emotion. You may have mixed feelings about selling what you've built; your M&A attorney won't.

5. *Wean yourself from involvement in the day-to-day operations of your company.* If you haven't begun doing this already (and you should have), start by delegating your duties to key managers. Hire someone if you need to. Forward 90 percent of your emails to others and let them respond. Stop going on sales calls. Start cutting your emotional ties as soon as you can. You don't want to find yourself killing a life-changing deal because you're overcome with seller's remorse.

6. *Consider whether you want to remain involved in the business in a reduced role.* There's nothing wrong with continuing to contribute to your company in some way, as long as you plan for it. Some entrepreneurs want to take some chips off the table but remain active in the company for a few years. You might do this by selling to a private equity group (which often requires the owner to stay on for five to seven years), or by selling to a strategic buyer and including a part-time consulting position in your contract. Just remember that you won't be the boss anymore.

7. *Talk privately to peers who have successfully navigated the change.* Other entrepreneurs who have gone from full-time entrepreneur to full-time sailor, golfer, or philanthropist

understand what you're feeling and can share their secrets for dealing with the fear, doubts, and sense of loss. They might even be a rich source of opportunities for new occupations such as charitable work. Just keep such conversations confidential; you don't want rumors circulating that you're planning to sell.

8. *Work with experts.* Figuring out what to do with the next stage of life is a huge task for men and women who for years had the discipline to focus on one thing: growing their business. Suddenly, they're adrift in a sea of financial questions, opportunities, resources, charitable organizations, and more, and it's overwhelming. By working with professionals who assist people in making the transition from working life to service life, you'll get help in dealing with emotional baggage, making better sense of your options, and gaining a clearer perspective on what comes next.

9. *Tend to your relationships.* Some business owners who spend more time at work than at home with family members tell themselves, "I'll give them all my time when I'm retired." But after decades of neglect, you might reach retirement only to find out that your family members don't want to spend time with you. Your spouse, kids, and friends are the people who will travel the next stage of life with you; start nurturing those relationships now. Don't wait for your exit.

The time after your exit from your business can be the most restorative, creative, productive, and rewarding years of your life. All it takes to make that happen is some forethought, some planning, and the right people on your team.

If you're close to your exit and you haven't given any thought to what you'll do after you sell, you might find yourself feeling a bit panicked. Relax, and cut to the chase by working with an organization that can help you manage the transition from working life to post-work life. You can also turn to peer groups for high-net-worth individuals facing transitions. Two of these are the Institute for Private Investors (www.memberlink .net) and TIGER 21 (www.tiger21.com).

Did You Know . . . ?

If you decide to go back into business after retirement, you'll have plenty of company. Recent research by the Ewing Marion Kauffman Foundation found that retirement-age people are starting businesses at the fastest clip of any age group. Its *Kauffman Index of Entrepreneurial Activity*, released in April 2013, revealed that people between ages fifty-five and sixty-four started 23 percent of the new businesses in the previous twelve months. That was actually *higher* than the percentage of businesses launched by the much younger age group.[32] In fact, an AARP survey found that nearly a quarter of self-employed people are sixty years old and older.[33] Experience pays off.

YOUR EXIT-PLAN CHECKLIST

You now know everything you need to start developing your exit plan. From here, the process becomes about taking three crucial steps:

1. Assemble your exit-planning team.

2. Create a comprehensive, cohesive financial plan.

3. Begin planning your exit.

Let's recap all the important to-dos and explore some parting advice. You can treat this as a checklist to guide your progress through the exit-planning process.

I. ASSEMBLE YOUR EXIT-PLANNING TEAM

First, choose your quarterback. That's generally always your financial advisor, and I suggest choosing a CERTIFIED FINANCIAL PLANNER™ professional (CFP® professional) to handle your financial planning on all fronts: investing, taxes, insurance, estate planning, charitable giving, and so on. To receive their certification, CFP® professionals have to meet the most rigorous training and testing standards in the financial industry. Your CFP® professional will be your number-one ally in the exit-planning process.

Beyond your financial advisor, you'll need the following professionals:

» A certified public accountant

» An attorney with mergers and acquisitions experience

» An investment banker with business sale experience

I strongly recommend going with an investment banker rather than a business broker. Business brokers typically sell very small companies, and many do little to create a stronger demand for your business the way an investment banker will, through the active solicitation of qualified buyers. Don't be seduced by the lower cost of a broker; you will almost always come out ahead, despite the larger commission, by using an experienced investment banker.

2. CREATE A COMPREHENSIVE, COHESIVE FINANCIAL PLAN

Before you can firm up your exit plan, you need a financial plan. Creating your plan will give you a clearer idea of what your business might sell for and how much work you have to do in order to achieve the post-work income you'll need to support your lifestyle. With your team in place, start working with your financial advisor to check off the following:

» *A business valuation.* Your financial advisor should give you a current open market valuation of your company at the beginning of this process. Until you know what you could sell for today, you can't know what steps are needed to generate the income you'll need.

» *Your personal wealth plan.* This will be your soup-to-nuts blueprint for asset management, investments, tax minimization, estate planning, insurance, charitable giving, and more.

» *A value driver analysis.* Based on the current sellable value of your company and the price you need to get in order to fund your lifestyle, your financial advisor and the rest of your team will recommend taking steps to increase the value of your company. Your value drivers might include putting systems and processes in place, removing yourself from day-to-day operations, acquiring a competitor, or numerous other strategic moves.

» *Your money "buckets."* You and your advisor will decide how much of your final liquidity event will go into your "nest egg" bucket (off limits to risky ventures) and how much will go into your "risky business venture" bucket, which you can use to do things like start another business or invest in an existing company.

3. BEGIN PLANNING YOUR EXIT

After you have your financial plan in place, start contemplating how you would like your exit to unfold. Key questions to ask yourself:

» When would you like to exit?

» How would you like to exit (e.g., selling to a third party, passing your business to family)?

» How much would you like to sell your business for?

» Would you like to be involved in the business after selling? If so, how?

» What would you like to do with your life after selling?

» What will occupy your time when you're no longer running a business?

» What percentage of your current income do you think you'll need to enjoy the lifestyle that you have in mind?

» How much, beyond the value of your business, have you saved toward retirement?

After you answer those questions on your own, it's time to sit down with your financial advisor to talk about the answers and your exit plan. Check off the important points as you develop your plan:

» *Know how you'll hit your value drivers.* What checks, systems, and processes are in place to ensure that you're growing your company's sellable value? Do you have a plan to pay down debt? Are you having your legal counsel review all contracts to make sure a buyer doesn't get stuck with burdensome commitments or expensive litigation? Do you have a plan for being less involved in everyday operations?

» *Attend to the basics.* Value drivers are important, but you've still got to take care of the essentials that make your company attractive to buyers. Have a solid, well-trained management team with a good incentive package. Make sure your financials are clean and in accordance with GAAP standards. Have a written, updated policies-and-procedures manual that can instruct a buyer how to do everything from backing up sensitive files to following up with prospective customers.

» *Have your acceptable deal in mind.* Don't wait until you're at the negotiating table to decide on acceptable financial terms. What's the lowest price you'll accept for your company? Will you offer seller financing? Will you accept profit sharing or earn-outs as part of your deal, even though they reduce the size of your liquidity event? If you decide that earn-outs are acceptable, treat them as bonus money. Don't formulate your financial plan based on a $500,000 earn-out windfall when you might be lucky to get $50,000.

» *Plan for the nonfinancial details of your deal.* Is your company incorporated in the way that allows the optimal financial return? Are you willing to work for the acquiring company? If so, for how long? Are you willing to sign a noncompete agreement? What terms would you find acceptable? What terms are unacceptable?

» *Have your post-exit financial strategy ready.* After a successful sale, you will probably have more money in the bank than you have ever had in your life. How will you manage it wisely? How will you handle requests from family and friends? How will you reconcile your newfound wealth with your children or grandchildren? How will you give back to the community?

WALK AWAY WEALTHY

Exiting the business you've worked so hard to build can be a challenging, emotional experience. It can also be the gateway to the life you've been waiting to enjoy ever since you opened your doors. Follow the steps and secrets I've outlined, and start now. It's never too early to build a leaner, smarter, more efficient business. In fact, the same principles that make a business more sellable also make it more profitable and enjoyable should you decide to hold on to it instead of selling.

Start today! Whether you exit next year, five years from now, or in twenty years, the sooner you start planning, the better prepared you'll be. Regardless of your exit path, I wish you a profitable and fulfilling future—and hope you walk away wealthy.

ENDNOTES

1 BizBuySell, 2013 Q3 Insight Report, http://www.bizbuysell.com/news/media_insight.html.

2 PriceWaterhouseCoopers, *Choosing Your Next Big Bet*, PwC Family Business Survey 2010/11, http://www.pwc.com/en_US/us/private-company-services/assets/pwc-family-business-survey-us-report-2010-11.pdf.

3 Tim Nguyen, in discussion with the author, October 2012.

4 Debra Repko, in discussion with the author, September 2012.

5 Cory Janssen, in discussion with the author, January 2013.

6 Manta, "Summertime Blues: Small Business Owners Working More with Less," news release, July 17, 2012, http://www.manta.com/media/q2_wellness_index_071612.

7 Josh Sanburn, "Staying Home: Fewer Small Business Owners Are Taking Vacations This Summer," *Time*, June 1, 2011, http://business.time.com/2011/06/01/staying-home-fewer-small-business-owners-are-taking-vacations-this-summer.

8   Josh Patrick, "Five Things About Passive Ownership
    You Need to Know," the Stage 2 Planning Partners blog,
    http://www.stage2planning.com/blog/bid/54130/
    Five-Things-About-Passive-Ownership-You-Need-To-Know.

9   Kurt Noer, in discussion with the author, January 2013.

10 Jim Krampen, "Want Decreased Health Care Costs and More
    Productive Employees? Send Them on Vacation," Inside INdiana
    Business, http://www.insideindianabusiness.com/contributors.
    asp?id=1301.

11 Deloitte, *Middle Market M&A News*, December 2012, http://
    www.deloitte.com/assets/Dcom-UnitedStates-CorporateFinance/
    Local%20Assets/Documents/us_dcf_middle_market_ma_news
    _december_2012_120312.pdf.

12 "How an Employee Stock Ownership Plan (ESOP) Works,"
    the National Center for Employee Ownership, accessed
    November 20, 2013, http://www.nceo.org/articles/
    esop-employee-stock-ownership-plan.

13 Brad Rosenberg, in discussion with the author, May 2013.

14 Merrill Lynch, *Affluent Insights Survey*, September 2012, http://
    www.wealthmanagement.ml.com/wm/Pages/Affluent-Insights-
    Survey.aspx.

15 *Life After an Exit: How Entrepreneurs Transition to the Next Stage*,
    prepared by Eugene Lang Entrepreneurship Center at Columbia
    Business School for Credit Suisse, 2011, http://www4.gsb.
    columbia.edu/filemgr?file_id=7217585.

16 Maeghan Ouimet, "Why Entrepreneurs Fail at Retirement,"
    Inc., December 2012/January 2013, http://www.inc.com/
    magazine/201212/maeghan-ouimet-why-entrepreneurs-fail-at-
    retirement.html.

17 Dave Zimmel, "Plan Now to Avoid Poverty," ProfitGuide.com, September 18, 2012, http://www.profitguide.com/prosper/plan-now-to-avoid-poverty-40944.

18 Melanie Hicken, "Don't Panic! Selling Now Could Hurt Your Nest Egg," *Time*, June 21, 2013, http://money.cnn.com/2013/06/21/pf/expert/market-selling.

19 Jules H. Lichtenstein, *Saving for Retirement: A Look at Small Business Owners*, US Small Business Administration, March 2010, http://www.sba.gov/sites/default/files/rs362tot_2.pdf.

20 Mark Miller, "Here Come the Boomer Biz Owners," WealthManagement.com, January 11, 2013, http://wealthmanagement.com/retirement-planning/here-come-boomer-biz-owners.

21 Mike Tucci, in discussion with the author, August 2013.

22 *Life After an Exit: How Entrepreneurs Transition to the Next Stage.*

23 "Ben Horowitz MS '90," UCLA Engineering alumnus profile, accessed November 20, 2013, http://www.engineer.ucla.edu/visitor-links/alumni/alumni-profiles-1/ben-horowitz-ms-201990.

24 Max Nisen, "Why Most People Fail At Launching Their Second Companies," *Business Insider*, November 27, 2012, www.businessinsider.com/why-second-startups-fail-2012-11#ixzz2kjCSkUsD.

25 David Einstein, "The Magic of Failure," *San Francisco Chronicle*, October 1, 1998, www.sfgate.com/business/article/THE-MAGIC-OF-FAILURE-Kamran-Elahian-s-startup-2987662.php.

26 David Reske, in discussion with the author, March 2013.

27 *Life After an Exit: How Entrepreneurs Transition to the Next Stage.*

28   International Franchise Association, *The Economic Impact of Franchised Businesses: Volume III*, 2007, http://www.buildingopportunity.com/download/National%20Views.pdf.

29   Rothstein Kass, *The Solution is Simple: More Planning, Greater Success*, December 2012, http://www.rkco.com/getattachment/66785e06-e830-4708-845e-0d465b911b32/More-Planning-Greater-Success.

30   Jeff Spadafora, in discussion with the author, March 2013.

31   David J. Linden, "Addictive Personality? You Might be a Leader," *New York Times*, July 23, 2011, http://www.nytimes.com/2011/07/24/opinion/sunday/24addicts.html?_r=0.

32   Robert H. Fairlie, *Kauffman Index of Entrepreneurial Activity 1996–2012*, Ewing Marion Kauffman Foundation, April 2013, http://www.kauffman.org/~/media/kauffman_org/research%20reports%20and%20covers/2013/04/kiea_2013_report.pdf.

33   Julie Zissimopoulos and Lynn A. Karoly, *Work and Well-Being Among the Self-Employed at Older Ages*, AARP Public Policy Institute, 2007, http://www.rand.org/pubs/external_publications/EP20070217.html.

INDEX

ABOUT THE AUTHOR

Mark Tepper is president of Strategic Wealth Partners and one of its founding members. He specializes in the wealth management and financial planning needs of entrepreneurs. He has helped numerous entrepreneurs build the value of their businesses, develop strategic exit plans, and maximize proceeds post-sale.

A well-known financial commentator, Mark appears regularly on CNBC's *Squawk on the Street* and *Street Signs*, as well as FOX Business. He has been featured in *The Wall Street Journal, Kiplinger's*, and *CNN Money*. Mark previously hosted *The IRA Guru*, a popular weekly radio show.

Mark holds a BSBA in Finance from John Carroll University and is a CERTIFIED FINANCIAL PLANNER™ professional. He lives in Brecksville, Ohio, with his wife, Jamie; daughters, Cameran and Riley; son, Kellen; and their two dogs.